NOVGOROD

Dvina R.

Neman R.

Volga R.

Don R.

KIEV

Dnieper R.

WITHDRAWN

Danube R.

CONSTANTINOPLE

Tigris R.

Euphrates R.

BAGHDAD

DAMASCUS

JERUSALEM

Nile R.

CAIRO

0	100	200	300	400	500 km
	62	124	186	248	310 miles

Series director: Michel Pierre, Professor of History
Art director: Giampiero Caiti
Assistant art director: Christine Tonglet
Editor: Martine Prosper
Project editor for U.S. edition: Joanne Fink
Editor for U.S. edition: Ruth Marsh
English text consultant: Walter O. Moeller, Senior Professor,
  Temple University.
Maps: Michael Welply
Photographs: Cassochrome, C.G.V. and Wespin under the
  technical direction of Claude Duhem.

© 1986 by Casterman, originally published in French under the title
  L'Histoire des Hommes: L'Europe du Moyen Age.
© 1988 English text by Silver Burdett Press Inc.

Published pursuant to an agreement with Casterman, Paris.

First published in the United States in 1988
by Silver Burdett Press Inc.
Englewood Cliffs, New Jersey.

Printed in Belgium.

Library of Congress Cataloging-in-Publication Data

Sabbagh, Antoine.
    [Europe du Moyen Age. English]
    Europe in the Middle Ages/Antoine Sabbagh; English translation
by Anthea Ridett; illustrations by Morgan.
        p. cm.—(The Human story)
    Bibliography: p.
    Includes index.
    Summary: Describes in text and illustrations the history of Europe
during the Middle Ages with emphasis on the spiritual, social,
political, and cultural developments and changes.
    ISBN 0-382-09484-0
    1. Europe—History—476-1492—Juvenile literature. [1. Europe—
History—476-1492. 2. Civilization, Medieval.]   I. Morgan, ill.
II. Title.   III. Series: Histoire des hommes. English.
D117.S2313 1987
940.1—dc19   87-22900
                                                    CIP
                                                    AC

Picture credits

Silkeborg Museum, Denmark: page 8. Giraudon: pages 12, 22 (b
and t), 24-25, 26, 27, 37, 38(b), 46(t), 47, 48, 52(t), 57, 67, 68, 71, 72.
Lauros/Giraudon: pages 25(t), 34, 39(t), 56, 74. Bibliothèque
Nationale/Archives Casterman: pages 11, 14, 17, 20 (b and t), 28, 32,
41, 45, 55, 66, 69. Vu du ciel/Alain Perceval: pages 18-19. Michel
Pierre: page 30. Éditions du Seuil: page 31. Pierre Tetrel/Explorer:
page 38 (r). Jean-Michel Labat/Explorer: page 38 (t). Jean-Pierre
Courau/Explorer: page 39 (b). C.N.M.H.S./Spadem: page 40.
Everts/Rapho: pages 42, 46. Laurence Brun/Rapho: page 36.
Phelps/Rapho: page 77. Jean Dieuzaide: page 50. Faillet/Artephot:
pages 44, 46(b). Phédon Salou/Artephot: page 52(b). E.T.
Archive/Artephot: page 70. A.F. Kersting/Artephot: page 75.
Promophot/Artephot: page 70. Roger-Viollet: page 58. Scala: pages
62-63.

THE HUMAN STORY
EUROPE IN THE MIDDLE AGES

Antoine Sabbagh
English translation by Anthea Ridett
Illustrations by Morgan

Silver Burdett Press
Englewood Cliffs, New Jersey

CONTENTS

PREFACE

"The Middle Ages," is the name that has long been applied to the thousand years between the fall of the Roman Empire and the Renaissance. While it was a very long period in human history, it has a real unity and continuity.

At the start of the Middle Ages, there was the slow, patient labor of millions of peasants battling with nature to produce meager harvests from the soil. In the eleventh century times began to grow less hard, but in the fourteenth and fifteenth centuries progress was set back by the recurrence of terrible disasters—plagues, wars, and famines. During the Middle Ages Christianity became all important. Under the sign of the Cross a culture was woven, thread by thread, with its popes, monks, priests, churches, and chapels. It was a period when no one could escape the influence of the Church, and when everyone lived in perpetual fear of the Devil.

The medieval world was bounded by the southern Mediterranean, the Islamic countries, and the lands east of the Balkans, where the Eastern (Byzantine) Empire still survived. Within these boundaries Europe was forged, with peoples who shared the same beliefs and religion and battled with the same terrors. But within this unity lay the seeds of individual nations, with their separate kingdoms and peoples, which gradually shaped the Western world as we know it today.

THE PEASANTS OF EUROPE

After the collapse of the Roman Empire in the fifth century A.D., the peasant's daily activities—picking berries and wild plants, growing a little grain, and battling with nature almost barehanded—were centered on survival.

The only populated areas of Europe were a few isolated clearings, some fertile valleys, an occasional village, and the remains of Roman cities. Everywhere living conditions were precarious. Daily life was overshadowed by the fear of famine, anxiety about the harvest, and the threat of an epidemic. Disease was the last straw for men and women who were worn out and old at age thirty-five, and familiar with death from childhood.

Examination of skeletons found in medieval graves tells us that there was not a generation that did not experience hunger. Yet there were times when there was enough food. If nothing disrupted the sowing and reaping and if the weather was kind, peasants managed to get enough to eat. Bread and boiled cereals were still the basic foods; but there were eggs, too, and chickens, dried and salted fish, and sometimes even meat. And from time to time beer and wine were drunk with meals.

To survive, people grouped together in small communities; for better protection, they gathered around the local church or castle. When the territory allowed, as in the Latium region of Italy and Provence in the south of France, villages were built on heights, away from danger.

Around the year 1000 A.D., aided by some slight changes in climate, technological advances and the end of invasions led to changes in the lives of European peasants. Tens of thousands of new villages sprang up, and large tracts of land were cleared of trees or won from marshes and the sea. During the tenth and thirteenth centuries the European population grew steadily, increasing from 22 million in 950 to 70 million in 1250. But this growth was brutally checked in the fourteenth and fifteenth centuries by a recurrence of the famine, warfare, and plague that had been prevalent at the start of the Middle Ages. It was as if a thousand years of human labor had only served to ripen the harvest of Death. No one has better summed up the hard life of the medieval peasant than the chronicler Geoffroi de Troyes: "The peasants who labor for everyone, who are always tired, through all the seasons, are constantly under pressure. They are harassed by fire, rape, and the sword. They are thrown into prisons and in chains, or else they die a violent death through hunger."

Archaeologists have excavated many medieval graveyards. Studying the bones gives them a great deal of information about the men and women of those days—their height, their physical characteristics, and what kinds of deformities or diseases they may have suffered from. A discovery in Denmark has even enabled us to see the face of a man from those days. "Tollund man," found in May 1950 in a peat bog, lived during the Roman Empire or early Middle Ages. His body, dressed only in a cap and leather belt, had been exceptionally well preserved in its burial medium of peat. He had a cord tied tightly around his neck. Was he the victim of a ritual murder, or was he a criminal, hanged after a trial? We shall never know the secret of this man, whose face has all the serenity of someone asleep for eternity.

A VARIETY OF LANDSCAPES

The peasants of the West, who made up 80 percent of the total population of Europe, lived in a variety of geographical and climatic conditions. In the south, the Mediterranean area was the realm of vineyards, cornfields, and olive groves and there were a few sparse, scattered forests of green oak. In the west, along the Atlantic coast, stretched heathlands and forests of oak and beech. These two trees could be found all over the Continent, but in the east they tended to give way to elms and birches. Pines grew mainly in Scotland and Scandinavia; they had not yet been introduced elsewhere.

The interior of a rural home. The earthen floor has a fireplace built directly into it, and no chimney. There are a few crudely made pieces of furniture. Men, women, children, and animals all lived in this one-room house, with its thatched roof and walls made of twigs and branches. However, in some parts of Europe, including the south, Greco-Roman building techniques had been passed down, and houses were built in well-cut stone.

THE LORDS OF THE EARTH

The real wealth of the Middle Ages belonged to those who owned land, whether provinces or small estates. All over Europe, kings, princes, counts, abbots, lords, and barons, who had acquired property over the centuries by combat or inheritance, dominated the peasants who tilled the fields.

Rural domains usually consisted of two parts, the demesne, directly maintained by the lord, and holdings leased to the peasants, in return for payments of produce, money, and services, all of which went to benefit the lord's demesne. The rents and duties imposed by the lord varied considerably between one domain and the next, and between one lord and his neighbor. Thus in the eleventh century Wulfardus, a tenant of the Abbey of St. Germain des Prés near Paris, had to work in the demesne twice a year, in winter and in March. He also had to cut trees, transport wine and wood when requested, and hand over three hens and fifteen eggs a year. Elsewhere, for example in a German domain of the twelfth century, every family had to give "4 hens and 10 eggs on St. Adolph's Day. . . . At Christmas, 12 loaves, 8 hams, a bucket of beer, and 4 measures of hay."

In exchange for protecting their peasants, the lords imposed further duties, such as cleaning the castle moat and supplying food and fodder to the castle garrison. Empowered by his position of command, the lord had the right to police his land and preside over courts of law. He collected tolls at bridges and fords, controlled markets and fairs, and levied taxes from tradesmen. Peasants were obliged to use the lord's mills and ovens to grind corn and bake bread, for which they had to pay fees.

In the twelfth century, agricultural advances brought about some changes in this system. Labor was no longer as useful as money. Some of the feudal nobles led lives of luxury, and they had to pay for costly military equipment and the expenses of warfare and crusading. Many of them fell into debt. At such times they would sell charters of freedom to the peasant communities for very large sums: instead of paying their dues in produce and services, the tenants had to pay money at certain fixed dates. As a result, the peasant communities began to be less cohesive and more self-sufficient. A minority of farm workers did very well, usually those who owned a cart and a draft animal, and especially those who lived in villages near market towns where they could easily sell their surplus farming produce. Alongside these well-off peasants, the poorer ones fell into debt or hired themselves out for seasonal work. The establishment of an economy based on money was one of the greatest social transformations in the history of the Middle Ages.

The steward, or bailiff, played a vital role in the lord's domain. In his master's name he organized the labor on the demesne, assigned duties, and levied taxes. He was also in charge of the castle supplies, and saw to it that tolls were collected and fees paid for the use of mills and ovens. Some stewards and their masters were so heavy-handed that they provoked violent reactions. But sedition was cruelly suppressed by the knights and their men-at-arms, who would hang, massacre, or mutilate entire village populations.

SERFS AND TENANTS

Peasants in the West did not all live under the same conditions. Some were free men who owned their own plots of land. They were called alleutiers *in France and* socmen *in England. Their freedom, however, was limited by the power of the local lord, who could exercise legal powers, owned the bakehouses and windmills, and levied tolls on roads and bridges. Tenants who leased land from a lord were also free, but they had to pay for the use of their fields in produce and labor. Serfs had the hardest time. They were tied to the land they tilled and could not leave it without the lord's permission. They also needed his permission to marry, and when they inherited a field there was a heavy tax to pay.*

The rights of the lords and the duties of peasants were gradually fixed and recorded in registers called "customals," in which were recorded the annual dues of money or produce that each peasant had to pay. Payment in kind could consist of one sheaf of corn out of 4, 5, 10, or 12 sheaves, a part of the grape harvest, or so many chickens and eggs. Peasants also had to pay tithes to the Church, usually consisting of one-tenth of the harvest, as well as regular monetary taxes levied by the lord. (Miniature from a fifteenth century manuscript, The Book of Rural Profits, Bibliothèque de l'Arsenal, Paris.)

WORKING THE SOIL

For medieval peasants the soil gave poor returns; it was infertile and difficult to work, submitting with reluctance to man's endeavors. Farming tools were primitive and inefficient. The ancient swing plow, with its wooden handle hardened by heat, barely scratched the surface of the soil and therefore, the furrows it dug were not very deep. Often, after the initial harrowing, clods of earth had to be broken up by hand to make it fine enough for the sowing. Tools for weeding, pulling up nettles, thistles, and wild plants were very crude.

It was impossible to do anything to improve the soil. There was not much to fertilize it with—just the clay and lime soil called marl, rotted leaves and grass, and straw left after the harvest. There was little or no manure; the herds were not large enough, though every animal dropping was carefully collected, as were the droppings of doves in the dovecotes, or roosts. Some lords demanded a precious "pot of dung" as part of their tenants' rent. This natural form of fertilizer was usually used on the castle kitchen garden and flower beds. Large fields remained as they were.

Badly worked and unfertilized as it was, the soil soon became exhausted of the nutrients that are so important to ensure plant growth. Thus, it had to be left to lie fallow, sometimes for one year out of two. Often it was so poor that it had to be abandoned for several years. In some regions, there were fields that produced only three harvests over a period of thirty years! Crop yields were pitifully small in spite of the large amounts of time and effort peasants put into work on them.

As there was little in the way of trade, each village and hamlet had to be self-sufficient, and grow some of everything. They had to produce barley, wheat, oats, vegetables, and wine, whatever the composition or state of the soil. So, out of necessity, grapes were grown in less than ideal conditions, far to the north of grape-growing country today. Vineyards were to be found in Brittany, England, northern France, and most all of the area in and around Paris.

A peasant's wealth was often reckoned by the number of iron tools he owned. Metal was rare and very expensive. But without iron plowshares, shovels, spades, sickles, and scythes, it was difficult to prepare the soil for good harvests.

If the young men of the village disapproved of a marriage—between an old man and a young girl, for instance—they would dress up in costumes and masks and gather outside the bridal couple's house. There they would show their disapproval by making a great deal of noise with drums, bells, and even cooking pots. There were other forms of celebration that carried on the old pagan traditions, such as the bonfires that greeted the arrival of summer on St. John's Day. Christmas celebrations were inspired by the ancient Roman festival of the sol invictus, *marking the winter solstice. (Bibliothèque Nationale, Paris.)*

The Middle Ages: an agricultural period made up of patient waiting, never-ending work, and ever-present worries.

The life of peasants was slow-moving, in rhythm with the cycle of the sun and the seasons. In December the pig was killed: sausages, bacon, and ham had to be prepared for the entire cold season. The icy hoarfrosts of January kept the peasants huddled around their smoky hearths. Work did not start again until March. The soil had to be dug, the plots sown with barley or oats, and the vines cut. The cattle were led out to graze peacefully on the fallow fields, while around the growing crops fences made of branches protected the young shoots from animals. The hardest times were in June, when fodder

was stored up for the winter, and the fallow fields plowed for the autumn sowing. This was the time when food stores were getting low, and it could be difficult to bridge the gap before the next harvest. At last came July, when the peasants reaped the grain with sickles, cutting it at mid-height, leaving the stalks to feed the animals. In August they threshed the corn with flails to separate the chaff from the grain. In October came the important task of grape picking. Then there was the final plowing before the corn seeds were sown for the following year.

There were scores of religious festivals, which tied

in with the rhythm of the seasons. As many as possible were held between Christmas and Easter, the period when there was the least work. For example, in order not to disrupt the farming calendar, at the end of the eighth century the pope moved All Saints' Day from May 13 to November 1.

This was the ideal rhythm of rural life, but it was often hampered by rain, hail, storms, and ice. Then the vines suffered, the corn rotted on the stalk, fruit trees were destroyed, and the harvest was endangered. Famine once again stalked the land.

THE FOREST

Around the villages the first cultivated pieces of land were vegetable plots, and around them lay the grainfields. A little farther away grew the forests, vast and impenetrable. Their dense growth of trees and plants encircled the hamlets that nestled in the hearts of clearings. The forest was an integral part of peasant existence, providing berries, wild fruits, acorns and chestnuts, and of course, honey.

The forest was also a source of tree bark. Peasants collected the bark to make shoes and baskets, resin for their lamps, healing herbs, kindling for their fires, and beams for their houses. In the very heart of the forest, charcoal makers prepared the fuel for the smith and the potter. And in the forest lived hermits, paupers, runaway serfs, robbers, and brigands.

Little by little the peasants cut away at the edges of the great woodlands, and burned larger clearings. The crops grown on these burned areas produced harvests that were ten times the normal size—for a year or two. In the eleventh century, the population was larger and the need for land greater, so as much forest land was cleared as possible. Among those wielding spades and axes were monks. The landholders—monasteries as well as lords—were all in favor of this expansion, which increased the size of their properties and brought in more rents. The great monastic orders of the twelfth century encouraged peasants to come and turn their forests into fields. Along the roads opened up through the woods, new hamlets, villages, and towns sprang up, which for a time were exempt from paying dues. With an economic leap forward in the thirteenth century, the great stretches of European forest land were replaced by vines and by large areas of fields. In the towns, great cathedrals were being built, requiring the felling of even more timber. Between the ninth and the fourteenth centuries the forestlands of France shrank by two-thirds. It was at this point that kings and lords decided to restrict the exploitation of woodland. They imposed taxes on tree felling and limited the use of the land for pasture, and especially for hunting. The forest was reserved for those in power, and became an area apart—an area that had to be protected and well-cared for.

Charcoal was essential. To make it, charcoal burners prepared a large stack of dry wood with an airhole in the middle and covered the stack with a layer of grass and ashes. Then they pushed burning sticks down the hole and sealed the stack to make it airtight. The stack was left to smoulder slowly for a period of from 2 to 10 days.

Stripping an oak tree. The inner side of the bark, rich in tannin, was used for making leather.

Cutting strips of wood to make barrels.

THE ACORN HARVEST

The forest, with its supply of wild berries and leaves, was the chief source of food for pigs, goats, and geese. There were acorns, too, which the swineherd would knock down from oak trees with a stick, as shown in this miniature taken from a thirteenth-century manuscript. (Bibliothèque Nationale, Paris.)

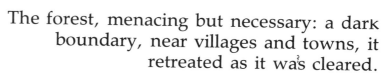

The forest, menacing but necessary: a dark boundary, near villages and towns, it retreated as it was cleared.

In the Middle Ages the wild cherry tree was protected so that the poor could eat its fruit. But the trees became so numerous that in France in 1669 a royal ordinance almost led to their extinction.

Woodcutters were both feared and respected; they played an important role in country life. They had a superb knowledge of the trees of the forest and understood its secrets.

THE TERRORS OF DAILY LIFE

"From famine, pestilence, and war, Good Lord, deliver us!" So humble people prayed for protection against their greatest fear, the return of the three evils that regularly struck down the men and women of the Middle Ages. It was a period fraught with uncertainty; people's lives were haunted by a thousand fears, scarcely alleviated by the occasional merrymaking at village festivals. One source of anxiety was the wildness of nature—the great unpopulated tracts of land, the deep forests, and above all the sea brought panic to the bravest heart. The rustling of leaves and the murmuring waters of a river spoke of the presence of supernatural beings that could drive human beings mad. As a precaution, until the twelfth century the homes of both rich and poor were built with few doors and windows.

As dusk fell, castle drawbridges were raised and the towns closed their heavy gates. People were sheltered from the fearsome world of darkness, when the Devil and his creatures walked abroad. At dawn, the terrors of the night fled at the first cock's crow. Only the monks, who prayed through the night, braved the darkness. Thus, medieval men and women lived in perpetual fear of Satan and his cohorts, and looked for help to the angels and saints. St. Martin was reputed to be the cleverest and most skillful warrior in the battle against Evil. On one side raged the evil world of demons; on the other the emissaries of God fought to free good Christians from their persecutors. Together they formed an invisible universe that was as real to believers as the visible world about them.

Little by little the peasants pushed back the bounds of the wild, but they still feared nature. A slight change in the weather before harvest time could be a disaster. Prayers were said for rain, since drought, which brought famine in its wake, was seen as punishment from God. People were fearful and suspicious of others—the neighbor who might have an evil eye, the soldier out for what he could get, the passing stranger. Lepers aroused special terror, for their diseased bodies were a clear reminder of the punishment that could be inflicted on sinners. Fear of outsiders arose from insecurity: bands of Normans, Moslems, and Hungarians continued to make raids until the tenth century, while in the fourteenth and fifteenth centuries bandits and mercenaries were still ravaging the countryside.

In this stressful atmosphere, the Church offered protection, and explained the daily terrors as traps Satan and his followers set for Christians. And who were considered Satan's followers? They were sorcerers, necromancers, heretics, and infidels—and all were shunned by society.

There were numbers of brigands and vagabonds in the forests, sometimes very close to the main towns. In the twelfth century, the French Bishop Suger wrote in a chronicle: "We founded a village at Vaucresson, we built there a church and a house, and we broke with the plow earth that had never been cultivated. This place was like a robbers' cave . . . a nest of brigands and vagabonds, because of the nearby woods."

THE YEAR ONE THOUSAND

As the year 1000 approached, some of the clergy believed that the world was about to end and that the Last Judgment would soon take place. Was it not written in the Bible that at the end of a thousand years, Satan, released from his prison, would go forth and seduce the nations in the four corners of the earth? People watched the skies and some believed they witnessed signs and portents of the end of the world. But this foreboding only affected a small minority. In the year 1000 means of communication were limited; Europe had few roads or towns, and the Western world was populated by tribes, peasants, and minor kings who believed in witchcraft and magic and were scarcely touched by Christianity.

Throughout the Middle Ages, famines and epidemics took a heavy toll of the population. In 1033 a monk called Glaber described the ravages caused by hunger: ''The corpses of the dead, which were so many that they had to be abandoned here and there without burial, became provender [food] for the wolves, and for a long time they continued to seek their prey amongst men.''

The medieval countryside had a large population of wolves, and this is commemorated in many place-names. In France the names Louviers and La Louvière, for instance, come from loup, the French word for wolf. Near towns and villages they were a real scourge. Attacks by wolves are mentioned in the Journal d'un bourgeois de Paris (Journal of a Burger of Paris) in 1438, 1439, and 1440. People tried various ways of trapping them. In the snare shown here, the wolf was lured by the scent of a carcass and fell into a pit, where it was captured alive. (Miniature from Book of the Hunt by Gaston Phébus, 1391, Bibliothèque Nationale, Paris.) Wolves disappeared from England in the thirteenth century. Their extinction was partly accounted for by a special dispensation by which exiled gentlemen were allowed to return home provided they killed a large number of wolves. Some killed as many as a hundred. To prove they had done it, they had to produce the heads of the slain animals.

GRADUAL PROGRESS

Until the year 1000, the tools that peasants used scarcely changed. Spades and hoes were still made of wood. Even on great domains, such as Annappes in the French province of Artois, iron was rarely used; the only metal objects were a few caldrons (kettles), two scythes, and two sickles. Only the lightest soils could be plowed. The rich, heavy soils of northern Europe remained uncultivated. To turn over the clay would have required heavy iron plows, so far only known to the Slavs. Draft animals were few, and they soon grew exhausted as they pulled on the collars around their necks, harnassed in an ancient method that threatened them with strangulation.

The first signs of change came in the eleventh century. Advances in the manufacture of weapons led to advances in metalworking as a whole. Forges were set up, and the peasants were equipped with metal axes, shovels, and spades. Use of the heavy plow slowly became more widespread, with its iron coulter that cut deeply into the soil and the addition of a moldboard that produced furrows. Draft and pack animals were shod; oxen were harnessed with yokes, and horses with padded shoulder collars that tripled their pulling power.

Land that until now was untouched could be cultivated. In eastern Europe, the Germanic princes offered inducements to settlers to come and clear their forests. From Flanders to Lombardy, marshes were drained. The best land, regularly worked over and better aerated, could now be left fallow only one year in three and planted with alternating crops of wheat in the winter and cereals in the spring.

Between the ninth and twelfth centuries the produce of the land almost doubled. The peasants' lot improved. To meet the demand from the growing towns, new crops were grown—vegetables, flax, and dye plants for the textile trade. Animal husbandry took a major leap forward. In England the great monasteries were surrounded by green meadows, grazed by long-fleeced sheep that sold for high prices.

The developments in farming and food production were reflected in commerce. There was a thriving trade in olive oil and spices, and particularly salt, extracted from salt marshes and salt mines. Salt enabled people to preserve meat, butter, cheese, and fish.

CHANGES IN CLIMATE

During the Middle Ages, the climate changed. There was a cool period, which lasted until 750; between the eighth and twelfth centuries it became slightly warmer—by about half a degree. This was enough to produce a noticeable improvement in harvests and a measurable increase in the population. In the thirteenth century a cooler period began, which lasted until the end of the fourteenth century. Areas covered with glaciers and snow areas grew larger. Norwegian settlers had to leave Greenland because of the cold. In Paris, during the icy winters, axes were used to break up frozen wine. In the fifteenth century another warm period began, which contributed to the lessening of famine at the end of the Middle Ages.

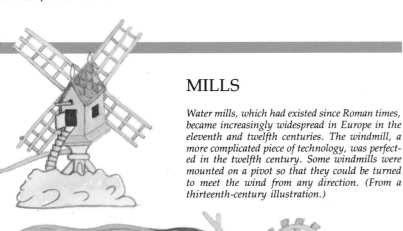

MILLS

Water mills, which had existed since Roman times, became increasingly widespread in Europe in the eleventh and twelfth centuries. The windmill, a more complicated piece of technology, was perfected in the twelfth century. Some windmills were mounted on a pivot so that they could be turned to meet the wind from any direction. (From a thirteenth-century illustration.)

The whole existence of the medieval peasants was devoted to working the land whose fertility had to be unceasingly replenished. The introduction of heavier, stronger, and more efficient tools helped to expand agricultural production. The method of hitching animals to plows and wagons also helped improve the food supply: the horse collar now rested on the shoulders and the chest of the animal, a big improvement over the earlier choke collar.

In the eleventh century, peasants acquired new tools that began to change the face of Europe.

An aerial view of Oise, in northern France, showing the clearings made during the Middle Ages. In the eleventh century, groups of peasants all over Europe began draining marshes and reclaiming land by building dykes. They attacked heaths and woodlands and the edges of forests; the forests themselves were indispensable to human existence, and they left them undisturbed. With their axes and plows they cleared acres of new land.

The wheeled plow, with its mobile front axle and iron plowshare with moldboard, enabled laborers to plow deeper furrows and prepare the soil thoroughly before the sowing.

THE FEUDAL SYSTEM

With the insecurities of daily life, bloodthirsty incursions by the Vikings in the west, Hungarian invasions in the east, and Saracen raids from the south, Europe was badly in need of protection. Not even the kings of Europe's many kingdoms were strong enough to defend the rural populations of the West. In the troubled periods of the ninth and tenth centuries, people put more faith in local chieftains who had real power in the form of fortified castles, and experience in commanding well-armed soldiers. Free men began to gather around these lords and their castles.

Little by little, independent communities organized themselves within territories of varying sizes. The lords' domains were like very small states, with all the power in the hands of one man. And while peasants all lived under similar conditions and formed one large class, the owners of lands and castles built up a new, complex system of hierarchical relationships. Everything revolved around a vast network based on the ties of vassalage. Under this system, called feudalism, those lords who were less rich and powerful, called vassals, swore oaths of loyalty to the more powerful, who became their overlords. The alliance between them was consolidated in the granting of the fief, a piece of land given to the vassals, and in their oath of allegiance. With this oath the vassal became the overlord's "man." In return for his lord's protection, he pledged him various services, most of which were military.

In this way, hundreds of vassals became independent rulers of their own fiefs. The fief became "noble land" and acquiring it was a sign that a man belonged to the nobility. Thus these noblemen found their place in a social structure that was gradually being defined by the Church. In the 900's the people of western Europe consisted of three groups: the noblemen, who governed the large fiefs and did all the fighting; the clergy, who served the Church; the peasants, who worked the land to support themselves, the clergy, and the lords.

The feudal system spread rapidly through the north of France, Germany, and, after the Norman Conquest, through England. It did not last as long in Italy, where the cities acquired more power than the nobility.

"Among the hooves of horses you will find the valiant." The tournament was a very important event in the Middle Ages. Hundreds of knights came with their squires, together with a throng of low-born contestants skilled at unseating riders with pike and lance. News of a large tournament drew crowds from all directions—not only lords and ladies, but horse dealers, prostitutes, and money changers, always on the lookout for a chance to do business. (Miniature from the manuscript of Tristan en prose, (The Prose Tristan), 1463, Bibliothèque Nationale, Paris.)

The act of homage (from the word homme, *meaning "man"). The vassal placed his hands between those of his lord, and gave himself to him—hence the expression "to be in good hands." The vassal swore: "Sire, I become your man," and the lord answered: "I receive you and take you as a man." After the oath of loyalty, the lord embraced his vassal and signified that he had granted him a fief by giving him a clod of earth, a ring, or a banner. (Miniature from a codex of feudal law, 1442, Bibliothèque Nationale, Paris.)*

For members of the nobility, hunting was at once an enjoyable pastime and a useful form of military training, providing practice in handling arms and controlling horses. It was also a means of obtaining fresh meat—venison was highly prized at lordly dinner tables. Hunting dangerous animals also provided an opportunity to exercise skill, self-control, and courage.

In the hunting world the art of falconry had a special place; it was a sign of wealth and power. Capturing and training falcons for hunting was a very costly sport, and keeping them required the permanent presence of a skilled falconer. Noble ladies enjoyed hunting with falcons, a sport that demanded no physical strength and did not end with a bloodthirsty kill.

THE POPE
AND THE BISHOPS

The medieval Church, confident that it alone was in possession of the truth and duty bound to reveal it to God's people, sought to impose its authority throughout the West. In the sixth century Pope Gregory the Great claimed direct descent from St. Peter, the founder of the early Church.

For centuries the papal monarchs worked hard to extend their authority over all believers—peasants and princes, kings and commoners alike. The papacy pronounced upon dogma and doctrine, founded and supervised universities, authorized the creation of new monastic orders, created dioceses, and proposed new saints for its flock to worship and emulate. It was also the papacy's task to ensure that the Church had an income. The nomination of the pope himself was not a matter for secular authorities. In 1059 Pope Nicholas II ruled that the election of the pope should be decided by the cardinals, meeting in secret. Regular Church councils were held to make decisions on legal and disciplinary aspects of Christianity. Such was the Second Lateran Council in 1139, when the Holy See forbade priests to marry, obliging them to remain celibate.

In every land the clergy tried to assert their independence from civil authorities. Sometimes they even clashed with kings, which could have its risks. In 1170, when his Archbishop of Canterbury, Thomas à Becket, questioned his decisions, King Henry II of England exclaimed, ''What idle and miserable and faithless men do I keep about me, who let me be mocked by a low-born clerk! Will no one rid me of this turbulent priest?'' To the king's later regret, four of his knights set off to Canterbury and murdered Thomas inside his cathedral.

In France, too, the kings became irritated by the pope's efforts to intervene in the government of their state. King Philip the Fair engaged in a violent quarrel with Pope Boniface VIII, who proclaimed the supremacy of spiritual over secular power. The conflict ended in the pope's humiliation. He was taken prisoner and exiled from Italy; he settled in the French city of Avignon, where the papacy had its home between 1305 and 1376. The defeat of Boniface VIII marked the end of the wordly ambitions of the medieval papacy.

This fifteenth-century German engraving shows Bishop Bruno visiting a cathedral site and blessing the masons. Building cathedrals could cost considerable sums of money, but the bishops had plenty of funds at their disposal—from bequests, alms, tithes, and royal gifts.

At Rome in 326 the emperor Constantine began building a basilica, on the site of the tomb of St. Peter. It was subsequently enlarged and added to by various popes until the sixteenth century, when it was replaced by the present St. Peter's. Perpetuating the memory of the chief apostle in this way confirmed Rome's position as the capital of the Church. In the words of St. Leo the Great (Pope Leo I): ''The apostles have raised Rome to such glory that it has become a holy place, an elected people, a sacred and royal city and the head of the world, thanks to the seat of St. Peter.''

When circumstances required, bishops and cardinals met to examine particular aspects of Christian belief and dogma or to discuss the organization of the Church. These councils were often attended by the pope. Any decisions made at these meetings entered into canon law and could be applied to the whole religious community. Thus the Fourth Lateran Council (1215) obliged Christians to attend annual Communion at Easter, forbade trial by combat and ordeal, and organized instruction. But it failed to carry out propositions for major reforms within the church. (''The Pope blessing the Cardinals,'' miniature from Les Riches heures du duc de Berry, Musée Condé, Chantilly.)

The popes, heirs to St. Peter, prince of the apostles, were conscious of their divine mission. They aimed to impose their authority throughout the whole Christian world.

In 1077 the German emperor Henry IV waited for three days and three nights outside the residence of Pope Gregory VII at Canossa, near Reggio Emilia, in northern Italy. The pope savored his victory: here was the proud prince, kneeling in the freezing cold, no longer insulting St. Peter's successor but begging for his forgiveness. For many years the German emperor and the pope had been engaged in the "War of the Investitures," concerning who should appoint the bishops and abbots of the great empire. In fact, this religious dispute masked a political question: Who was the real ruler of western Christendom—the pope or the emperor?

Gregory VII excommunicated the rebel emperor, depriving him of spiritual authority. Disavowed by the Church, threatened by his own people, Henry IV resigned himself to this humiliation, but plotted his revenge. Seven years later he took it by seizing Rome.

DREAMS
OF EMPIRE

Among the Germanic tribes who had overturned the Roman world in the fifth century were the Franks. Three centuries later the imagination of the Frankish princes began to be fired by the power and grandeur of the Roman Empire, which had lasted over four centuries. Their own power was limited to small territories, and their authority was often challenged. They began dreaming of the times when an emperor reigned over the undivided area of the Atlantic to the Danube, from North Africa to Asia Minor. With the idea of reviving these great days, Pepin the Short turned to the Church for support, and recognized the pope as political ruler of Rome. The resulting alliance was a great advantage to his son, Charlemagne, who was crowned king in the year 800. Charlemagne saw himself as the representative of God on earth, battled against the pagans, and tried to endow his court at Aix-la-Chapelle with all the splendor of ancient Rome. But he remained primarily king of the Franks, and never planned to found a dynasty that would continue to rule over the lands he conquered. After his death, the division of these lands and the Viking invasions brought his empire (known as the Carolingian Empire) to an end.

However, Charlemagne's deeds remained alive in peoples' memories, and some Germanic princes gradually revived the idea of an empire. In 962 Otto I was crowned Holy Roman Emperor by the pope after vanquishing the Hungarians who had been threatening western Christendom to the east. The ceremony sealed the alliance between the pope and the prince who had saved the Christian world. But Otto's successors only ruled over German territories, and their "imperial power" was ignored by powerful princes like the kings of France. Despite many long struggles and offensives, they never managed to extend their power beyond the Rhine and to the south of the Alps toward Italy, so often the target of the desire for conquest. In the thirteenth century, after the death of Frederick II, the king of Germany, the emperor's ambitions were confined to ruling over Germany. In 1344 the imperial throne even lost its hereditary nature and became elective. At a meeting in Frankfurt, seven German princes were appointed as electors. The dreams of empire faded; the desire to unite the whole of Christendom had failed. Although rulers continued to adopt the prestigious title of Holy Roman Emperor, none of the other kings recognized them as having any authority, for "every sovereign is emperor in his kingdom."

Only in the East, on the banks of the Bosphorus, was the heritage of Rome carried on. Since the fifth century the Byzantine emperor, in his capital of Constantinople, had declared himself to be the true successor of the Roman emperors. He reigned over the most splendid city in Europe, possessed unheard-of riches, and controlled a powerful fleet. He was in fact the most formidable ruler of the Middle Ages. For centuries the Byzantine Empire withstood all attacks. But in 1204 it fell victim to the greed of the knights of the Fourth Crusade, one of a series of holy wars against the Moslems. Although it was reborn from the ashes, it was permanently weakened, and was captured by the Turks in 1453.

In the Middle Ages the heritage of Rome was kept alive at Constantinople. The Basileus *(the emperor) was regarded there as a sacred figure, head of both Church and State. Gradually separated from the West by a religious quarrel that led to a schism in 1054, Western Christendom regarded him with a kind of fascinated horror, and gave him no help when the Mussulman Turks (Moslems) invaded Constantinople in 1453. (The Empress Theodora, 527–548, mosaic from San Vitale, Ravenna.)*

On December 25, 800, Charlemagne was crowned emperor at Rome. Pope Leo III placed the crown on his head to the acclamations of the crowd. ''To Charles Augustus, great and pacific emperor, long life and victory!''

With this gesture the pope hoped that Rome would return to its former place as capital of the empire. But the Frankish emperor chose to settle at Aix-la-Chapelle, where he had a palace built. The palace was designed to imitate that of the Byzantine emperor, whom he recognized as ruler of the eastern territories.

Artists enjoyed representing the emperor on his throne. He is shown here wearing a crown and holding in his right hand a globe, symbol of his authority over the whole world. In his left hand is the scepter of command, which was sometimes topped with the ''hand of justice,'' symbolizing the power of life and death over all his subjects. Finally, draped in a cloak embroidered with all the constellations in the sky, the emperor is made to appear as a superior being, invested with magical powers. (Musée Condé, Chantilly.)

THE KINGDOMS OF EUROPE

In the year 1000 the West was divided into a multitude of domains, duchies, and towns that were more or less independent. It hardly seemed ripe for large kingdoms to take shape. However, by the end of the eleventh century the English and French monarchies were to assert their power over the turbulent feudal society. The first condition for a royal house to be independent was recognition of its hereditary nature. In France, Hugh Capet, a descendant of the counts of Paris, was elected king in 987; during his lifetime he succeeded in getting his son accepted as the rightful heir to the throne. All his successors did likewise, until Philip Augustus (1180–1223). The Capetian family line was solidly established and when a related family, the Valois, took the throne in 1328, the changeover took place without disturbance. Similarly, in England, the descendants of William the Conqueror were followed by the Plantagenets.

At first the kings had to ensure the obedience of the feudal lords, their most powerful vassals. At his accession, Hugh Capet only exercised authority over his own domain, the Ile de France, which his successors made every effort to enlarge. By means of intrigues, alliances, and the constant support of the Church, they gradually managed to eat away at the territories of the large landowners.

Kings also had to make sure that they had an effective government and that royal justice was supreme. At the same time, they had to ensure themselves of an income and select royal agents to carry out their decisions. In all these things the king of England succeeded earlier than did the king of France. On the death of England's King, Henry II, in 1189, the monarch ruled over the entire country. This was several decades before the Capetians (Philip Augustus, St. Louis, and Philip the Fair) made much progress in this domain in France. At the beginning of the thirteenth century, when King John signed the Magna Carta in 1215, giving the barons a say in the government, England was the most modern and stable of the Christian states. That is why, although it had a population of barely four million, it was able to oppose the French colossus, with its fourteen million souls, in the Hundred Years' War.

THE DIVINE RIGHT OF KINGS

In all the countries of Christian Europe the power of kings was recognized as having a divine origin. "The King is beholden to no man save God and himself," it was said at the court of France.

The act of consecration symbolized this recognition. The king received the crown, ring, and scepter—religious symbols—alongside the military symbols of spurs and the sword. Blessed by the Church and sanctified by the bishop, it was the king's duty to defend the Christian faith and to rule over his subjects according to Christian ideals of justice and charity. In the Middle Ages the man who best lived up to this ideal was St. Louis, king of France from 1226 to 1270. (National Archives, Paris.)

On July 27, 1214 at Bouvines, between Lille and Valenciennes, after bitter fighting, the troops of King Philip Augustus of France defeated the armies of the German emperor Otto IV and his allies, the count of Flanders and the king of England. Wild celebrations greeted the victor's return under the sign of the royal banner with its fleur-de-lis. The victory enhanced the prestige of the French crown and rallied to the king's side many formerly hesitant vassals. To his people, the king appeared as the protector of his country against the enemy threat.

Monarchies were often forged out of the heat of struggle. The kingdoms of Spain—Castile, Aragon, and Navarre—were born out of battles against the Moslems. In central Europe, the kings of Poland, Hungary, and Bohemia had to confront the Germans, bent on conquest.

In Scandinavia a Danish empire and a Norwegian kingdom were created; Olaf Haraldson of Norway (995–1030) was the first Christian monarch. After his death, pilgrims flocked to worship at his tomb; when miracles began happening there, the Church declared him a saint.

In the fourteenth century, when the Scandinavians were trying to free themselves from the economic domination of the Hanseatic League, King Olaf became a national hero and patron saint of Norway. (Wooden statuette from the parish church of Valö in Sweden.)

A PASSION FOR WARFARE

In the thirteenth century a troubadour, Bertran de Born, sang of the delights of war: "I tell you this: nothing has more savor for me, neither eating, nor drinking, nor sleeping, than to hear the cry of 'Forward!' " A band of knights charging with their lances pointing straight ahead was an awesome sight to the footsoldiers watching the wave of steel unfurl to the heavy galloping rhythm of powerful horses. With their shields decorated with dragons and lions, their clanking armor, and fearsome-looking helmets, the cavalrymen must have resembled demons from Hell. Footsoldiers were simple peasants, unable to afford horses or equipment like the hauberk, the long tunic made of chain mail—thirty thousand metal rings linked together. They protected themselves by wearing hemp-lined tunics and by carrying a pike or an ax to unseat horsemen. Once grounded, the knight's armor, weighing about 40 pounds, made him clumsy and much less powerful. The footsoldier could remove his helmet or slip a knife between the chinks in his armor. Similarly, skillful archers could halt a cavalry charge by wounding the horses. But during the incessant fighting of feudal times, real battles were rare events. They were highlights in the struggles between two powerful adversaries, both of whom submitted to the judgment of God. On the few occasions when battles did take place, they brought together thousands of combatants. At Bouvines in 1214, 4,000 riders and 12,000 footsoldiers clashed. And since a captured knight could be worth a good ransom, each side took care not to injure the other too seriously. Warfare was primarily a way to make money and prove one's valor, rather than exterminate the enemy. At Bouvines only two knights were brought down, one by accident. But no one bothered to count the number of low-born corpses. They were not interested in these victims of war.

Aside from major confrontations that decided the future of dynasties and powerful families, military operations most often consisted of disorganized skirmishes, besieging castles, or capturing towns with the help of traitors rather than by vigorous attacks. Wars were fought only in the summer, and no one had the means to employ armed soldiers all year round. Only the king of England, in the thirteenth century, maintained a professional army, and even this was not large. In the rest of Europe it was the knights, from the most powerful to the most humble, who responded to their king's call to arms.

As large kingdoms took shape, the art of warfare changed. Collective tactics became more important than individual deeds. The kings, aiming to wipe out their adversaries, encouraged the development of new weaponry.

In the fourteenth century the English and the Italians perfected a bronze tube into which gunpowder was inserted. When this was ignited, the explosion caused a heavy projectile to be ejected. The cannon had been born. It was heavy, expensive, and not very accurate, but it had a terrifying effect. Cannonballs broke up cavalry charges and broke down the walls of fortresses. (Chroniques d'Angleterre [Chronicles of England] by Jean Wavrin, fifteenth century, Bibliothèque Nationale, Paris.)

THE MILITARY IDEAL OF CHIVALRY

At the age of 10 a knight-to-be could ride well. On horseback he knew how to tilt his lance at the quintain—a dummy fixed on a wooden frame set up in the castle courtyard. To complete his education, his father would send him to be a squire to another lord, where he would learn how to handle a heavy sword. At 15, after giving proof of his valor, he was dubbed a knight. The ceremony of dubbing took place in the presence of his father's vassals. The young man was presented with a sword, and a knight placed a well-aimed blow on his shoulder, the "accolade," with his hand or sword. If his father was rich enough, he could buy a horse and armor. His dream was fulfilled: he could leap onto his destrier, his powerful warhorse, and ride off in search of adventure.

In the eleventh century the Church took it upon itself to curb the aggressive spirit of the knights. By the "Truce of God" it forbade fighting on holy days and between Wednesday evening and Monday morning. Dubbing became a religious ceremony: the priest blessed the knight's weapons, and the knight, who had spent the previous night in prayer, swore to protect the weak and the Church. Knights became warriors of God, model Christians who were depicted on the façades of cathedrals.

Knights were, understandably, very proud of their military prowess and sought opportunities to display their courage. For one-to-one fighting they needed heavy suits of armor. The body was protected by a chain-mail tunic, the hauberk, and the head by a metal helm or helmet that covered the entire skull. Plate armor appeared in the fifteenth century, but the high cost of iron and the time it took to make meant that a suit of armor was a real luxury, for wealthy noblemen only. Ordinary horsemen wore leather jerkins and a small leather or iron cap, or casque. Swords, lances, and of course horses were indispensable.

Many of the early castles were made of wood, but from the eleventh century on, solid stone fortresses were built, with ramparts reinforced by turrets. Machicolations and loopholes (small openings) were built into the walls and floors wherever possible through which to shower the enemy with arrows and stones. If the castle did not succumb to a surprise attack or trickery, a siege would ensue. The attackers would try to burn down the castle door, but did not often risk climbing the walls with ladders. Kings often had an impressive array of siege equipment. They could break down ramparts with trebuchets and catapults, throwing machines that could hurl huge boulders. Flaming arrows, shot from enormous crossbows, could land inside the castle. Attackers also used towers on wheels, carrying soldiers and weapons. These towers could be placed up against the castle wall. When their doors were opened, the soldiers inside them poured out into the castle. Another, less risky solution was to wait until the defenders ran out of food and water. When they lowered the drawbridge to get out, the attackers could gain access to the castle.

Types of helmets worn by ordinary soldiers

During a siege, the attackers would undermine the castle walls. Under cover of night they would dig a tunnel at the foot of the walls where the stonework was loose. They would shore up the mine with timbers then set them ablaze. The fire would bring down a section of the ramparts, and the soldiers could then get through the breach.

29

CHRISTIANITY AND THE CHURCHES

The Europe of the Middle Ages was the Europe of Christ's Cross. It was formed around churches, chapels, cathedrals, and monasteries. The barbarian tribes who had overturned the Roman world in the fifth century had become converted to Christianity. In 496 Clovis was the first ruler of the Germanic tribe of Franks to be baptized. Rome, the ancient capital of the empire, now became the seat of the pope.

After resisting the attacks of the Moslems in the eighth century, Christendom—the Christian world—set out to enlarge its frontiers and defend itself against the brutal incursions of pagan invaders like the Normans and the Hungarians.

Christianity began to spread westward. St. Boniface preached the Gospel in Germany, while Charlemagne used fire and the sword to convert Saxony to the religion of Christ. But the most remarkable conversions were those of the barbarian princes, together with their entire peoples. They included Boris, khan of the Bulgars in 864, and Vladimir, prince of Russia, who became a Christian in 988 through the influence of missionaries from Byzantium. From his capital of Kiev, the Byzantine form of Christianity spread slowly among the Slavic tribes of the Dnieper and the Volga regions. Missionaries from Rome converted the Croats and Slovenes and in 963 began their evangelical work in Poland. At the beginning of the eleventh century, bishoprics were established in Scandinavia and even in Iceland. From then on, from Europe to the Volga, from the Baltic to the Mediterranean, millions of men and women theoretically worshiped the same God.

But, in many regions, the conversions to Christianity only existed on the surface. Pagan practices, witchcraft, and magical rites did not die out. In 973 a great insurrection of the Slavs was followed by the disappearance of the organized Church between the Elbe and the Oder. In 1038 the people of Poland rebelled in favor of paganism, and two years later the powerful movement they had started hit Hungary. Local people had often been forced into Christianity by their newly converted rulers, and they revolted against those who had destroyed the shrines of their gods, broken their idols, and denied their ancestral beliefs.

The fabric of Christianity was weakened when the Christians of East and West parted company in the Schism of 1054. The Eastern Church, proclaiming itself to be the orthodox church that respected the true faith, gathered around the patriarch in Constantinople. In the West, Christians remained faithful to the pope, the bishop of Rome: they called themselves Catholics, from the Latin word *catholicus*, meaning "universal."

Born of the fusion of the Roman world and the migrations of the Franks, the Western world of the Middle Ages gradually took on a character of its own. This cemetery in the French town of Civaux, watched over by a ninth-century church, symbolizes the slow development of medieval culture. In these stone coffins rest the descendants of the Frankish warriors who had gradually overtaken the Roman Empire and given birth to a new civilization.

THE SCHISM WITH THE EAST

In the seventh century a bitter power struggle took place in central Europe between the missionaries of the Roman and Greek churches. It reflected the secular quarrels between the religious authorities of the two ancient imperial capitals, Rome and Byzantium. The patriarch of Constantinople and the pope in Rome were in conflict about the interpretation of religious texts, differences in ritual, and questions of precedence. In 867 a pope and a patriarch mutually condemned each other to divine execration. In the two centuries that followed, there was no lessening of the conflict. In 1054 the rupture became permanent, when Pope Leo IX excommunicated the patriarch Michael Cerularius.

In the middle of the ninth century, two Greek monks, Cyril and Methodius, set out to convert the pagans of central Europe to Christianity. To make themselves understood, they worked out an alphabet derived from the Greek. These "Cyrillic" letters enabled them to translate sacred texts into the Slavic dialects. Other Greek missionaries converted the Slavs who settled in the Balkans, the Serbs, and the Bosnians.

On their faraway island, away from migrations and invasions, the Irish monks preserved the heritage of the early Christians. Around 590, St. Columban, a monk from the monastery of Bangor, landed in Britanny. He was followed by hundreds of Irish monks who traveled all over the Continent, founding monasteries as far away as Switzerland, Germany, and northern Italy. Their names crop up today in hundreds of place-names, particularly in Brittany, on the coastal regions of the Atlantic and the Channel.

MONKS AND MONASTERIES

There were some Christians who faithfully followed Christ's commandments as recorded in St. Matthew's Gospel: "If thou wilt be perfect, go and sell what thou hast, and give to the poor, . . . and come and follow me." They became hermits and monks, men who lived apart. One of the first was St. Anthony who, in the third century, lived in solitude of the Egyptian deserts before founding a community.

After this, other communities were formed, and from its beginnings in the East the monastic movement spread throughout the West. Disciples would gather around a holy, pious man, and dedicate their lives to acting out their faith in prayer and total poverty. The barbarian invasions during the fifth century actually made the monastic movement stronger. In a brutal world, many believers saw a life of prayer and meditation as the only means of preserving the purity of their souls and assuring their salvation.

At the beginning of the sixth century, St. Benedict of Nursia enlarged the scope of monasticism. In 529 he founded the Monastery of Monte Cassino, in the Apennine mountains of Italy, where he imposed a strict rule. The monks, who were all ordained priests, tried to achieve an ideal of Christian perfection by practicing obedience, chastity, and humility, and devoting their lives to work and prayer. A few decades later, the Benedictine Rule became general all over Europe. In a world beset by savagery and violence, thousands of Christians became monks, inspired by St. Benedict's message. The monasteries they founded were genuine islands of peace, work, and prayer, unique centers of religious influence, where the abbots exercised their authority with moderation and a gentle spirit.

Monks played an important role in the history of the Middle Ages. As missionaries, they converted vast areas. As military men, like the Knights Templar, the Knights Hospitallers, and the Teutonic Knights, they carried the sword and the cross far to the east and south of Europe. With their knowledge of reading and writing, and their monastery libraries, they became guardians of culture. As builders, they created magnificent monasteries. They tilled the fields and tended the vines, and adopted new agricultural techniques, selecting and improving plants and vinestocks and developing animal husbandry. They also worked as weavers, smiths, and miners—and they provided the Church with a great number of extremely pious and morally upright popes and bishops.

In the monasteries, clerks had the important task of transcribing holy books. The first to excel in this art were the Irish; they produced some magnificent manuscripts decorated with scrolls, animals, and stylized human figures. Throughout the Middle Ages, the monasteries were active centers of art and culture. The richest owned up to 1,000 manuscripts, which they often lent for others to copy, thus preserving an invaluable cultural treasure. (Text with illuminated initials, Sacramentary and Martyrology of Gellone, end of the eighth century, Bibliothèque Nationale, Paris.)

FROM CLUNY TO CLAIRVAUX

In 910 the reforming Abbot Berno founded the Abbey of Cluny, in the French county of Mâcon, in order to restore the Benedictine Rule to its early purity. In the following decades, the Cluniac order, directly attached to the Holy See, expanded far and wide. In the eleventh century it had more than 1,100 monasteries in France, England, Spain, Poland, and even Scandinavia. Some were very beautiful and contained valuable ornaments. Other orders, such as the Cistercians in the Abbey of Cîteaux, reacted to all this wealth and power by seeking a return to the early monastic ideals of solitude and poverty. In the twelfth century there were more than 500 Cistercian monasteries in the West. An outstanding member of the Cistercian Order, who denounced the glories of Cluny Abbey, was St. Bernard (1090–1153); the abbey he founded at Clairvaux, in Champagne, was one of the most remarkable spiritual centers of medieval Christianity. Two centuries later, the mendicant orders— the Franciscans and Dominicans—dedicated themselves to preaching and teaching in the towns.

The Benedictine Rule ordered that the monk's life should include a balance of meditation, religious exercises, manual labor, intellectual pursuits, and the practice of Christian virtues. The Rule stated that "the monastery must be arranged in such a fashion that the basic needs can be met there: water, a mill, a garden, and workshops in which various trades can be practiced within the walls. The brothers must devote certain hours to working with their hands, and others to reading and holy matters." The abbot's duties are also mentioned, with an emphasis on the obedience that all the monks owe to him. "He who accepts the dignity of abbot must govern his followers with a double teaching, that is to say he must inculcate that which is good and healthy by his actions, even more than by his words . . . Everything must be done according to the abbot's will."

To distinguish one from another, the monastic orders adopted different colors. The Benedictines wore sackcloth-brown, and the Carthusians stood out in their white robes. The Franciscans remained faithful to the dark colors of the early monastic communities.

Franciscan   Cistercian   Benedictine   Carthusian   Dominican

WALKING FOR GOD

At the shrine of a saint, lamps would burn night and day as the pilgrims pressed around the tomb. Some of the sick were carried, too weak to walk. They would come with offerings of candles or pieces of cloth, or they would simply place their open palms on the stone tomb as if to absorb its miraculous properties. The reputation of each shrine depended on that of the saint and on the value and number of relics venerated there. All over the West people sought out the bones of the holy martyrs. Some people went so far as to ransack tombs and steal relics from one city to sell to another. Some of these remains had already traveled a long way. The relics of St. Mark the Evangelist, housed in Venice, had been brought from Alexandria in 823. At Bari, in Italy, people worshiped St. Nicholas, bishop of Myrsa in Asia Minor, whose remains had been brought over by sailors in 1087. All over Europe centers of pilgrimage sprang up. Pilgrims came to them to save their souls, to beg for a cure, or to fulfill a vow.

Going on a pilgrimage was also a way of doing penance, a means of purifying one's soul in preparation for the Last Judgment. And although its purpose was to prepare for the end of mortal life and the begining of life eternal, people also found it an enjoyable way of getting away from their everyday cares. They could set out on the road, see new countries and sights, and receive a welcome at monastery after monastery, where they would be fed, lodged, and given instruction. Thousands of Christians took the road every year to Rome, Jerusalem, Mont-Saint-Michel, and after the death of St. Thomas à Beckett, Canterbury. From the tenth century one of the most popular pilgrimages was to the shrine of St. James of Compostela, in northwestern Spain. People from all over Europe flocked to the "Field of the Star" (the name Compostela comes from the Latin *Campus Stellae*). A star was believed to have indicated the site of the apostle's tomb, where the basilica was built.

The pilgrims who took themselves to St. James's tomb all wore on their garments the famous cockleshell, which was his emblem. According to one legend, a knight who had been thrown into the sea by a frisky horse was rescued by St. James and came out of the water covered in shells. According to other legends, the body of St. James himself had been found covered in shells. Whatever the truth, the cockleshell made a handy cup for drinking water from springs and rivers, and it became the symbol of pilgrims.

A marvelous example of the craftsman's skill, this reliquary ornamented with gold and precious stones is a sumptuous container for the mortal remains of a saint. A reliquary is a small box, casket, or shrine in which relics are kept. They are sometimes covered in paintings illustrating the miracles and martyrdom of the saint. (Reliquary of St. Laurent, fifteenth century, Musée des Beaux-Arts, Moulins.)

The French village of Conques, lying on one of the main routes leading to Compostela, offered shelter to pilgrims in its huge church, built in the twelfth century. There they came to venerate a tenth-century statue of St. Foy, who was martyred at Agen at the end of the Roman Empire. This fabulous reliquary was covered in gold and jewels, and sometimes aroused the wrath of clerics who saw it as a sign of idolatry. But for the crowd of pilgrims, it was a dazzling object; it was only right that it should contain the precious relics of a victim for the faith.

THE CHRISTIAN CALENDAR

When a child was born the parents took it to the church to be baptized, and the church bells were rung to announce its entry into the Christian community. When anyone died a priest was summoned to administer the last sacrament. Over the newborn child and the dying person, the same sign was made—the sign of Christ's Cross. The Church's influence on everyday life was constant and absolute. The Church decided what foods one was permitted to eat; there were feast days and fast days according to the time of year. Eating pork during Lent or meat on a Friday were sins meriting severe punishment. The Church controlled the days and nights, too. From morning till evening the ringing of bells announced the succession of prayers and offices. At night the streets echoed with the voice of the town crier—"Awake, sleeping Christians, and pray for sinners!"

The great Christian festivals replaced the pagan feasts that had marked the seasons. Christmas was set on the date of a former sun festival, which had been celebrated around the winter solstice: the birth of Christ was surely the better symbol of the victory of light over darkness! The other great annual events took place according to the liturgical calendar. Easter, Ascension Day, Pentecost, All Saints' Day, and St. Michael's were not just religious festivals but important dates in economic life. They coincided with the days when farming rents and dues were paid, when craftsmen and workers had the day off.

Christ's protection also extended over particular places, held to be sacred, where acts of violence were not permitted. One was the village church; a runaway serf or a wanted criminal who could reach it and touch the door handle was safe from pursuers. The church was the heart of the community.

For the medieval man and woman, God was omnipresent—invisible but always there to protect or threaten. The Church was always on the watch for indications of the divine will. In the great battle against Satan and the forces of evil, its mission was to protect the faithful. With its rites, festivals, prayers, sacraments, and regular services, it ensured that every moment of every day was directed toward God.

A variety of processions and ceremonies marked the rhythm of the Christian year. During the three days before Ascension Day, the Rogations (from the ecclesiastical Latin, rogationes, meaning "requests" or "prayers") were held. Their object was to draw divine blessings down on the harvest and the tilling of the soil. In the Church calendar, the days were named in relation to the feast days of the great saints; people spoke not of "September 24" but "the fifth day before St. Michael." The four seasons and the twelve months corresponded with the four evangelists and the twelve apostles. Spring began at Easter, or St. George's Day, April 23. Summer began on St. John's Day, June 24, and winter on St. Martin's Day, November 11. Even the length of the hours varied: they were shorter in winter and longer in summer. No one had any idea that the earth revolved once on its axis every 24 hours and around the sun every 365 days. The earth was thought to be a flat disk covered by the vault of the sky through which the sun made its daily journey.

THE SAVIOR'S CROSS

In remote areas, and at crossroads, the Cross of salvation gave travelers reassurance. In the presence of the symbol of Christ, the world became less fearful; the powers of darkness had to withdraw and the demons hold back.

But feudal lords did not always respect the sanctity of the Cross. And when fugitives clung to the doors of churches, their hands were sometimes cut off so that their agonized bodies could be seized. (Thirteenth-century Cross at a crossroads on the Causse Méjean.)

The rhythm of the days was punctuated by prayers and services.

Until the eleventh century, weddings were performed without a priest, by mutual consent or parental pressure. In the following century, marriage became a sacrament. The Church ruled that a priest should unite the couple, joining their hands in a gesture of mutual giving. This gesture underscored the sacred and permanent nature of the marriage. The exchange of rings, which gradually became common practice, was borrowed by the Church from ancient Rome.

The sacrament of marriage had its opponents. In the second part of his Roman de la Rose (The Romance of the Rose), at the end of the thirteenth century, Jean de Meun launched into a virulent attack: ''Marriage is a detestable chain . . . Nature is not so crazy that she gives life to Marotte solely for Robichon, if we look well, nor Robichon for Marotte, nor for Agnes, nor for Perrette; nature made us all, fine young people, all maidens for all men, and all men for all maids.''

ROMANESQUE ART

At the beginning of the eleventh century the Burgundian chronicler Raoul Glaber wrote: "As the third year that followed the year One Thousand was approaching, almost over the whole earth, but above all in Italy and Gaul, the churches were re-built. . . . One might have thought that the earth was shaking itself to shed its skin, and was everywhere re-clad in a white coat of churches."

Townspeople, now richer and more numerous, founded new shrines to celebrate the glory of God; master masons and builders of genius expressed their faith in their offerings of stone. This religious preoccupation was encouraged by pilgrimages and the worship of relics, the devotion of monastic communities and the gifts of lords.

Church and cathedral walls were no longer made of unmatched materials smothered in mortar but of stones cut into regular-size blocks and fitted smoothly together. The walls, which were much more solid than before, could now be built higher to support a vault, or arched roof. The arch was the most important feature of Romanesque, or Norman, architecture, a style based on Roman architecture.

Inside the churches, at the transept (the part of a cross-shaped church at right angles to the long, main section, or nave), builders sometimes erected domes, which the ancient Romans were so skilled at building. The naves and aisles, apses (altar section) and choir were divided off by pillars. The tops of these pillars (the capitals) were sculpted with episodes from the Bible, Christian symbols, devilish monsters, and sometimes scenes from daily life. Outside, above the glorious entrance to the House of God, Christ was often depicted sitting in majesty among His saints at the Last Judgment.

Fine shafts of light penetrated the church through the aisle windows or, less often, through the high windows of the central nave. This gentle, diffused lighting gave Romanesque churches a unique atmosphere of peace and intimacy. By contrast, the pillars and capitals blazed with a myriad colors. All the sculptures were painted, as were some of the walls, which might otherwise be decorated with fabrics, frescoes, or rich tapestries.

The façade of the church of Notre-Dame-la-Grande à Poitiers (twelfth century), is an example of the decorative and symbolic richness of Romanesque buildings. On the second story a double row of statues of apostles and bishops frames a huge window, which diffuses the light inside the building. The center of the gable is ornamented with a mandora, *an almond-shaped niche in which Christ appears surrounded by the symbols of the evangelists.*

THE VIRGIN AND CHILD

Romanesque sculpture has a naive quality about it. The gestures are stiff, and human figures out of proportion, made to look squat or unrealistically long and thin. But from them emanates a sense of faith, a religious fervor, and a symbolic power that are quite inimitable.

The theme of the Virgin and Child became popular with the spread of the cult of the Virgin. The crowd of worshipers venerated the Mother of God enfolding her Son's body in her protective arms. On this casket, the infant Christ is holding up his hand in a gesture of blessing. (Musée des Beaux-Arts, Poitiers.)

The Abbey of St. Martin de Canigou was founded by the count of Cerdana in the early eleventh century. It was consecrated in November 1009 in honor of St. Martin, the Virgin Mary, and the Archangel St. Michael.

The building consists of two basilicas, one on top of the other. The lower church is dedicated to the Virgin Mary, who reigns in the shadow of the crypt, and the upper building to St. Martin. St. Michael, to whom people dedicated the upper parts of holy buildings, has his chapel in the nearby bell tower.

The architecture of both churches is very archaic in character, with huge pillars and barrel-vaulting throughout. Similar buildings had appeared in some provinces of the Byzantine Empire, notably in Greece and Asia Minor, several centuries earlier.

The capitals of Romanesque columns were like sculptured pictures, designed to instruct worshipers; they were composites of many styles. They included classical leaf decorations and scrolls, mythical monsters from barbarian times, elegant figures from Byzantium, and geometrical designs originating from Islamic countries. The iconography of Benedictine manuscripts was also reproduced in stone, which was covered with Latin inscriptions. These stone pictures taught the crowd of illiterate worshipers the stories of the Bible.

Every feature of a Romanesque building had a symbolic meaning. Churches were usually in the form of a cross, with the apse facing east, toward Jerusalem. The cloisters of monasteries were built in a square, reminding the monks of the world as a whole. Their four sides evoked the four points of the compass, the four elements of nature, the four branches of the cross, the four evangelists, and the four cardinal virtues. (Cloister of Moissac, twelfth century.)

HERETICS AND INFIDELS

Constantly anxious about the salvation of their souls, fearing both God and the Devil, and trying to understand the source of good and evil, the Christian community sought peace of mind in the rites and teachings of the Church. But these did not satisfy everyone's spiritual needs, and some people considered that the dogma proclaimed by the pope and bishops had little to do with the example set by Christ.

At the end of the tenth century the ragpickers of Milan started a revolt against the corrupt clergy and demanded that priests lead good lives in poverty. Similar demands were made a century later at Lyons, where a wealthy merchant, Peter Waldo, gave up everything to live in poverty according to the Gospels. His disciples, called Waldensians, criticized the wealth of the clergy and renounced their own goods to live by begging.

Another group of heretics, the Cathari, named after the Greek word for "the pure," made absolute purity their goal. They believed in the existence of two gods, a good god living in heaven, and a god of evil, who had created the world of matter. They believed that to save one's soul one must despise and renounce the material world. They rejected the sacraments and teachings of the Roman Church, but instituted a rite of spiritual baptism, the *consolamentum*. This rite separated "the Perfect," who were pledged to maintain absolute purity, from the ordinary believers, who had to strive to approach this ideal.

Little by little the Cathari faith became a real religion in opposition to the official Church. It affected people in both towns and country, clerics and great lords. It took lasting root in Provence and Languedoc, in southern France, and along the commercial routes leading to the Byzantine Empire. It became so widespread that in 1167 it held a great international council at St. Félix de Caraman, near Toulouse.

In the face of this challenge the papacy decided to stamp out the heresy by force. The pope organized a crusade, led by a French nobleman, Simon de Montfort, and made up of a number of minor nobles from northern France who were greedy for land and thirsty for bloodshed and pillage. During this "Albigensian Crusade" the town of Béziers was sacked in 1209, part of its population exterminated, and the Languedoc region laid to waste. But it was not until 1244 when the Château of Montségur, a Cathari stronghold, was captured that the Cathari resistance really came to an end.

The heretical movement of the Bogomils ("the beloved of God") started in Bulgaria in the tenth century. It was propagated through the Balkans before reaching the Byzantine Empire in the East and playing an important part in the birth of Catharism in the West.

The Bogomils rejected the sacraments and did not recognize the Old Testament. They preached a dualistic belief in a good god and an evil god who must be renounced by the "Perfect." (Coffin from a Bogomil cemetery, twelfth century, Herzegovina, now Yugoslavia.)

In the eleventh century anti-Semitism was unleashed in Europe. With the Peasants' Crusade, an enormous number of Jews were massacred. As a chronicler wrote: "They sincerely believed they were avenging Christ on pagans and Jews. That is why they killed nine hundred Jews in the town of Mayence, not sparing women and children . . . It was pitiful to see the many great heaps of bodies brought out of the town of Mayence on carts."

In the twelfth century the Jews were gradually deprived of the right to own land or practice any trade. Soon their only means of livelihood were on the illicit fringes of business and moneylending. They were regularly expelled from provinces and countries. Forced to make themselves recognizable, they attracted scorn and hatred. In Poland they had to wear green hats; in Germany, they wore red or yellow hats or symbols sewn onto their clothes. In the fourteenth century they were made to live in ghettos, special sections reserved for Jews alone. One of the first was in Venice, the Ghetto neighborhood from which we get the name.

Excluded from the Christian community,
heretics could expect nothing but suffering
and punishment.

To oppose the Cathari, the Church set up a tribunal
called the Holy Inquisition, which had the power to
arrest, try, and condemn heretics. The accused, ill-
treated and tortured, would confess to whatever the in-
quisitors wanted. After they had been condemned, the
Church handed them over to the secular authorities to
be punished—usually by burning at the stake.

John Huss, a Czech, demanded social justice, religious morality, the reform of the Church, and patriotism. He
was arrested and burned at the stake in 1415 by order of the Council of Constance. But his death was followed
by an uprising in Bohemia, and at the end of the "Hussite Wars" (1419–1437) the Church had to concede
to the Czechs some of the rights that Huss had demanded. (Bibliothèque Nationale, Paris.)

41

THE RECONQUISTA

arly in the eighth century, Spain was conquered by a Moslem army from North Africa. Thus began the rule of the Moslems, called the "Moors" in Spain. Their rulers, the caliphs, were all-powerful, exercising tolerant control over their Jewish and Christian subjects. In the north the principalities that were still Christian accepted the domination of Islam, the Moslem religion, and peace reigned.

After 980 the truce was broken by an Arab chieftain, Abu Amir al-Mansur, and Christian towns were regularly pillaged. Twenty years later, however, the situation was reversed. Al-Mansur was dead, and Moslem Spain was divided into rival principalities, while in the north the Christian monarchs united with the aim of achieving the *Reconquista* (the Spanish word for *reconquest*). Forgetting their temporary agreements with the Moslems, they banded against Islam. With the French princes as allies, and the support of the powerful Order of Cluny, they tightened their links with the rest of Christendom. The pilgrimages to Compostela brought warrior knights, eager to battle the infidel, to Spain. The pope himself incited the Christians of the West to fight against the Moslems in Spain.

In the second half of the eleventh century the Christians of Aragon and Castile moved to the offensive. In 1085 Toledo was captured. The Moslem rulers summoned formidable bands of warriors from Morocco to their aid. In tight ranks, marching to the beat of war drums, they shook the Christian knights but could not prevent their advance. The resistance produced a hero, Rodrigo Díaz de Vivar, whom the Moors nicknamed "El Cid" (Arabic for "The Lord"). He defended Valencia with great gallantry and was killed there in 1095.

For a whole century, Christian offensives alternated with counterattacks from the Moors. The Christians were divided among themselves. But on July 16, 1212 the kings of Castile, Aragon, and Navarre formed a temporary coalition and crushed the army of the caliph of Cordova at Las Navas de Tolosa. It was a decisive battle. Now nothing could stop the *Reconquista*. Cordova was captured in 1236, Seville in 1248. At the end of the thirteenth century, the Moslems only had control of the kingdom of Granada; there Islam was not to be driven out until the end of the fifteenth century.

In the middle of the eleventh century the Reconquista turned into a religious war, a holy war preparing the way for the spiritual and military philosophy that sent crusades to the Holy Land. It was led by Christian kings aided by mercenaries, knights from beyond the Pyrenees, and members of military orders like the Knights of St. John. The monks of Cluny, who had encouraged the pilgrimages to Compostela, also played an important part in the reconquest of Spain. A knight of the Order of St. James (thirteenth century).

THE LIONS OF GRANADA

At the end of the thirteenth century the Moslems' only remaining Spanish territory was the tiny kingdom of Granada (with some 400,000 inhabitants). There the arts, literature, and science were highly valued. The magnificence of the Alhambra (Arabic for "red") Palace illustrates the civilized culture enjoyed there. The Court of the Lions is surrounded by colonnades of white marble. In the center is a beautiful fountain supported by twelve stone lions.

Five centuries of struggle between Christendom and Islam for possession of Spain and Portugal.

The Reconquista was accompanied by a systematic program to repopulate and revive the country, which had been devastated by so much fighting. As each stage of the conquest was achieved, Christian peasant settlers were installed. Swords were replaced by plowshares. But the old tensions between the two communities often remained alive, and the Moslems, now under Christian domination, were not allowed freedom of worship and belief. At the end of the fifteenth century, after the capture of Granada, they were given the choice of converting to Christianity or leaving Spain.

SOLDIERS
OF CHRIST

After the year 1000 the fervor for making pilgrimages to the Holy Land increased. For thousands of Christians, visiting the very places where Christ had lived and suffered his Passion was the supreme goal, which would guarantee them eternal life. Since 636 Jerusalem had been occupied by the Moslems, but they did not prevent Christians from visiting the city. However, at the end of the tenth century the Seljuk Turks conquered the Middle East. News reached the West that the new conquerors were making life hard for Christian pilgrims and would soon forbid them access to the holy sites. The spirit of pilgrimage now changed to one of aggression. This was fostered by the papacy, which saw it as a way to use a knight's love of warfare by making them defenders of the faith against the infidels; the papacy seized this opportunity to unite Christendom in a Holy War against Islam.

In 1095 at Clermont, Pope Urban II preached the First Crusade. His appeal, relayed by popular preachers like Peter the Hermit, aroused a unanimous response. At the cry of "God wills it!" thousands of Christians sewed red crosses onto their garments, symbols of the Crusade. From the overpopulated country districts of Flanders, the Île de France, and even Scotland, entire villages joined Peter the Hermit's Peasant's Crusade. They set out for Jerusalem, heading east, believing daily that they were getting nearer to the Holy Land. Armed with axes and pikestaffs, these poor people crossed Europe in a mood of fanaticism, pillaging, and massacring. But none of them saw the Holy City. Many returned after months of marching in the wrong direction. Some groups reached Asia Minor but were killed there by the Turks in the autumn of 1096.

Meanwhile, another, better organized crusade had set out and three separate armies totaling 60,000 strong were converging on Constantinople. There were no kings or princes among the knights; they were the younger sons of nobles or knights who had got into debt, like Godefroy de Bouillon, who pledged his possessions to finance his journey. In the East their numbers were reduced by hunger, disease, and rivalry among themselves, as well as fighting. In July 1099 only 6,000 stood before Jerusalem—but fired with battle fury, they captured the city and wreaked horrible carnage among its inhabitants.

But those who were left behind after the first crusades were isolated, few in number, and received little in the way of reinforcements; they were unable to stand up to the Islamic counteroffensive. Little by little the Moslem vice closed in on them, and one by one the Christian states were wiped out. In 1187 Saladin, sultan of Syria and Egypt, took possession of Jerusalem. In response, the Third Crusade set out. Although it was led by three kings—Philip Augustus of France, Richard the Lion-Hearted of England, and the Holy Roman Emperor Frederick Barbarossa—they were unable to recapture the Holy City.

Although there were to be five more crusades, the failure of the Third Crusade marked the end of any hope of recovering the Holy Land. Many Christians were still inspired by dreams of reconquest, including St. Louis, King of France, who lost his life in 1270 in the Siege of Tunis in the Eighth Crusade. Twenty years later Acre, the last Christian fortress in Palestine, was captured by the Moslems.

Returning from the crusade

This wooden carving, in the Ropemakers' Chapel in Nancy, represents Count Hugh de Vaudémont on his return from the First Crusade, greeted affectionately by his wife. He is shown as a pilgrim, with a Cross hanging from his neck, the pilgrim's staff, and totally unmilitary clothing. His face seems to express extreme weariness after an adventure beset by so many hardships.

The Crusades did not satisfy the western Europeans' hunger for land, and brought nothing to Christendom—no increase in trade, no new techniques or products, none of the intellectual resources of the translation centers and libraries of Greece, Italy, and Spain. The only novelty introduced by the Crusades was the apricot, which was imported from the Middle East to be grown in the gardens of Europe.

The Holy Wars between Christians and Moslems sometimes led to scenes of terrible violence and savagery. According to a Crusader, at the capture of Jerusalem, ''there was such carnage that our men were walking in blood up to the ankles. . . They ran through the whole town, seizing gold, silver, horses and mules, and looting the houses.'' On the other side, a Moslem wrote: ''On Friday 22 Shaban [a month of the Moslem year] 492, the people were put to the sword and the Frankish massacre of the Muslims [Moslems] of the town went on for a week.''

But there were also many acts of chivalry between the Christians and the Islamic warriors, who are shown here on a fourteenth-century manuscript. (Miniature from a manuscript of the Roman de Godefroy de Bouillon, 1337, Bibliothèque Nationale, Paris.)

The wanderlust that gripped the Christians was partly satisfied by the Crusades, which promised everything—adventure, wealth, and the salvation of the soul! But the violence they unleashed affected everyone—Moslems and Jews, and the eastern Christians as well. During the Fourth Crusade in 1204, the Venetians diverted the attack against Constantinople. The town was captured and looted, and the Crusaders indulged in the worst excesses before turning it into a short-lived Roman Empire (1204–1261).

TEMPLES OF LIGHT

In the twelfth and thirteenth centuries a new style of architecture arose to express the faith—and the wealth—of the West, the style became known as Gothic. Gothic architecture had its beginnings in the Île de France. Its first great expression was the monastery church of St. Denis near Paris, which was renovated in 1140 under the direction of Abbot Suger. It was followed by a series of magnificent buildings in Laon, Paris, Chartres, Reims, Amiens, and Bourges. In the next century, French architects were in demand all over Europe, from England to Hungary and from Flanders to Spain.

Gothic architecture was a way of honoring God by offering Him a house radiant with light. Cathedrals were also symbolic representations of the light of religion, liberating souls from the darkness of evil. So they had to be built to immense heights, their walls pierced with as many windows as possible, filled with plain and stained glass, to flood the interior with color. To sustain the great heights of these cathedrals, more solid vaults had to be built. These vaults, supported by flying buttresses, became more pointed and lost their arched form.

But what this cathedral architecture primarily signified in Europe was the new prosperity of the towns. Craftsmen and merchants saw it as a symbol of their own work and of the money they donated toward the building of their church. They had pictures of their deeds reproduced in stained glass, together with the tools of their daily trade. Their guilds gathered in the huge naves, where there was room for the entire local population. The cathedral was the house of the townspeople. Rising over the narrow streets, houses, and squares of the city, the cathedral was the sacred center of the lives of the people. It was also a symbol of pride and wealth, a place where the congregation could meet and celebrate, and a gauge of the city's eternal renown.

When a community chose its emblem, or insignia, the most appropriate symbol of its power became the outline of the church dominating the town. An exaggerated example of this local pride, and the aim to outdo other cities, was Beauvais Cathedral. Its vaulting was the loftiest (157 feet) and the widest (52 feet) and it was given the largest windowed surface in France. It was built in 1272, and collapsed twelve years later. Although rebuilding was begun, it was never completed, for the cost would have been enormous in proportion to the city's resources.

Gothic sculpture is imbued with serenity, far from the often terrifying images of Romanesque art. A sly sense of humor and elements of satire sometimes crept in and are found in some depictions of the Last Judgment. Sculptors idealized their models, placing them in noble postures and dressing them in flowing drapery. The Virgin was given a round face and curving hips, and long, wavy hair. She held the infant Jesus, who is seated on her right arm or close to her in a comforting maternal pose. (Private collection.)

THE MASTERS OF GOTHIC ART

The architects and builders who first tried out their skills in the Île de France, cradle of the new style, were often invited abroad. A German memoir dated 1258 recounts that a prior "summoned a master mason highly skilled in architecture, and just arrived from Paris," and asked him to build a stone church. The most famous of these master builders was Villard de Honnecourt, an architect from the Cambrai region who traveled all over Europe. In 1235 he wrote a treatise that includes plans for a sanctuary, a tower, and a rose window, and designs for a Crucifixion and a Virgin for the stone carvers to use as models. He also drew everyday scenes—wrestlers, a man on horseback, a king and his consort, some astonishingly realistic animals and fabulous beasts, and geometrical designs. He invented a circular saw, designed a machine to lift heavy loads, an automaton, and even a metal sphere to keep a priest's hands warm!

The soaring lines of Gothic architecture, bathed in light, and the tall pillars, draw the eye up toward the intersecting ribs of the vault. The windows above the high galleries illuminate the nave and the choir, from which sacred music rises. In front of a chapel to the Virgin, a priest offers up the blessed Host for the worshipers to adore. In the center of this scene rises the Cross with the crucified Christ; at His feet St. John supports the Virgin, who has fainted. The God of justice of Romanesque times had been succeeded by God made Man, who suffered to pay for the sins of the world.

In this painting by Roger van der Weyden (1399–1464), a Flemish painter born in Tournai, Belgium, the cathedral acts as a frame for the ''Swooning of the Virgin.'' The expert use of color, dramatic composition and rendering of perspective make it a true masterpiece of Gothic painting. (Musée des Beaux-Arts, Antwerp.)

The building of Salisbury Cathedral in England was begun in 1220. Most of it was finished in 1266, and it was finally completed in 1284. The bell tower and its spire were added in the fourteenth century. The cathedral incorporates many features characteristic of Gothic architecture in full flower—the façade pierced with bays and niches containing statues, flying buttresses, a huge nave, and walls latticed with large windows.

SCHOLARSHIP AND UNIVERSITIES

The barbarian invasions and negative climate changes had swept away much of the culture of antiquity. Books and the written word held little interest for fighting men, hungry for land, bent on pillage and instant satisfaction. Only the monasteries preserved the writings of the saints and a few Greek and Latin manuscripts that had been rescued from destruction. In rooms called *scriptoria*, the monks copied the texts in superb manuscripts, destined for the treasuries of the churches rather than for general reading. Books were precious, in the same way a silver plate or golden chalice would be! However, under Charlemagne's rule, written culture was revived. The empire needed men who could read and write legal texts. But this "Carolingian Renaissance," as it was called, only affected a minority, the elite belonging to the palace.

It was not until the twelfth century that a new Western culture began to take form. The population growth, the expansion of trade, and the building of towns stimulated the exchange and movement of ideas. Men of learning, enriched by a knowledge of Greek and Arabic texts, rediscovered the authors of antiquity. They absorbed the new thinking alongside the lessons of the Bible and the teachings of the founding fathers of Christianity. Bernard of Chartres exclaimed: "We are dwarfs sitting on giants' shoulders. We can see more and further than they, not because we are taller or our eyes sharper, but because they carry us aloft and raise us to their full colossal height." And Pierre of Blois asserted: "We can only pass from the darkness of ignorance to the light of science if we re-read the works of the Ancients with ever keener love." Nurtured by this new culture, the masters changed their behavior and attitudes.

In Paris, Oxford, and Bologna, and all over Europe, universities were created, linked to the growth of towns and cities. Unlike the monastery schools, where the teaching was often rigid, they were true centers of learning attended by students from far and wide. The universities gradually acquired genuine autonomy. In 1231, after some bloody demonstrations and a long strike lasting over two years, St. Louis formally recognized the independence of the University of Paris. The masters who taught there were respected for their desire for knowledge, the depth of their religious thinking, and the freedom with which they conducted debates in an effort to reconcile logic with the teachings of the Church.

The Latin word *universitas* means "guild," and the masters, who were both teachers and scholars, banded together to form guilds to protect their rights. They lived on the money their students paid for lessons. Some were followed from town to town, regarded as true masters of thinking. Some universities were more highly regarded than others, and some became specialized. Bologna became famous for its law school, Montpellier and Salerno for their medical studies, and Paris for the study of theology and philosophy. An Englishman, John of Salisbury, wrote in 1164: "I have made a visit to Paris. When I saw there the abundance of food, the liveliness of the people, the consideration enjoyed by clerks, and the various activities of the philosophers, I thought I looked in wonderment at Jacob's ladder reaching to the sky with angels walking up and down on it."

In the Middle Ages education often consisted of a study of texts and "disputes" on their meaning, questions and interrogations on their hidden significance. Seated on a dais, the master read aloud, commented, and gave answers. Opposite him sat the students, who were often poor, particularly in the twelfth century. They had no permanent home and they went from town to town to get what education they could. Sometimes, to earn a living, they worked as jugglers or clowns, begged or stole. They sang songs of pleasure, drinking, and love. "I will die in the tavern: there, where the wines will be close to the mouth of the dying man. After the choirs of angels have come down singing: May God have mercy on this good drinker."

In the thirteenth century, as the universities became organized, these "goliards," as the wandering scholars were called, became fewer in number and the bands of lively witted travelers and vagabonds faded out. They were succeeded by students who were better off or given financial assistance by charitable institutions. Such an institution was the college founded by Robert de Sorbon in 1253 in Paris, which was to grow into the Sorbonne, the present-day University of Paris.

Alongside oral lessons, the basis of teaching became the written word. The authors on the syllabus had to be read by both masters and students, and records were kept of the professors' lectures. The book, once a luxury item, became a manual, a tool. Paper-making processes improved, books became smaller, abbreviations and a modern script came into use. Reeds were replaced by quill pens, which made it possible to copy manuscripts more speedily. This was appreciated by the impoverished students who copied them out for bookshops close to the universities.

The university consisted of four independent faculties. The arts faculty taught a six-year course and granted a bachelor's degree. Then came the specialized faculties—law and medicine—which granted students a doctor's degree. Theology, the most "noble" discipline, demanded from 15 to 16 additional years of study. A complicated examination system regulated the allocation of university grades. (Arithmetic, fifteenth-century engraving.)

THE ARABIAN HERITAGE

During the intellectual renaissance of the twelfth century, the Arabs served as intermediaries. Moslem schools and libraries were filled with the works of ancient Greece. These manuscripts traveled from the East through Italy and Spain to the West. Some original Arabic texts, Arabic versions of Greek texts, and original Greek texts were translated with the help of Spanish Christians who had lived under Moslem rule. It was a huge task, but little by little the cultural gaps left by the Latin heritage were filled. Research, logic, and science made enormous progress by contact with Euclid's mathematical works, Aristotle's philosophy, and Hippocrates' writings on medicine. In addition, the Arabs made their own contribution, including the writing of modern numerals and subjects such as algebra, agronomy (the science of crop production), and alchemy. In the twelfth century the Koran was even translated by order of Pierre the Venerable, Abbot of Cluny, to combat the "Mahometan error," as he called Islam, and to "recognize the enormity of this error and block its path."

ON THE RUINS OF THE ROMAN EMPIRE

Under the Roman Empire, town life had been the basis and mark of civilization. Besides being political, administrative, and military centers, towns also provided buildings for all kinds of pleasures and entertainments. After the fifth century, all that remained of the remarkable urban centers were skeletons of stone. The great buildings became places of refuge, were used as fortresses, or turned into dwelling places. The former temples became churches.

Tucked into corners of defensive walls that were now too large for them, some towns and cities survived because of their religious role. They were the seats of the bishops. The bishopric was the source of the town's sole economic activity—the granaries from which, in times of famine, food was distributed to the small population of clergy, soldiers, and artisans.

After the year 1000 urban life began to enjoy a slow revival. As the West became richer and better populated, trading increased, and the highways became busy once again. As the population grew, peasants were drawn to the towns and cities, where they could often find freedom from the landowners.

Soon the new townsfolk threw off the shackles of the feudal lords. The small towns they lived in were called *bourgs*, from which the English word *borough* is derived. These new middle classes demanded and often obtained charters of freedom, giving them the right to self-government in return for a regular payment. They were laying the foundations of a community spirit, in which townspeople would be linked by feelings of fraternity and near equality.

This urban growth, both in government and communal life, required the careful organization of tasks and the cooperation of citizens. Contrary to popularly held beliefs, most medieval cities were well-built and well-planned. They were dotted with squares and fountains and, since the cities were generally small, there was easy access to the open countryside outside the walls. Overcrowding, therefore, was not a great problem. In northern Europe the houses were built mostly of wood and plaster, while in southern Europe stone was more available. Where the cities had a large number of wooden houses, fires were frequent.

In the ruined cities of the Roman Empire, life began again. Large buildings like the Colosseum in Rome and the amphitheater of Nîmes were used as fortresses. Stones from other buildings were used as material for new buildings. Sometimes houses were built within the ruins of ancient places of entertainment, such as the Theater of Marcellus in Rome and the Amphitheater of Lucca in Italy. And ruins that were too big to be used were left to decay, while the herds cropped the grass around them. The magnificent Roman Forum became the campo vaccino, *the cows meadow.*

In the thirteenth and fourteenth centuries, in England and southwestern France, there was an unprecedented growth of new towns. In France, hundreds of bastides— small fortified market towns—were built by the counts of Toulouse and the kings of France. To encourage people to live there, feudal dues to the local lords were abolished, people and buildings were exempted from taxes, and the inhabitants were granted freedom to work the forest land.

The dead bones of the Roman cities flicker
back to life.

ROADS AND PORTS

Medieval society was far from sedentary. Men and women did not feel bound to their patch of land, nor did they limit their horizons to the neighboring woods. The roads were busy with knights, peasants, monks who traveled regularly or had broken with their monasteries, and students heading for schools and famous universities. And there were pilgrims, vagabonds, and beggars everywhere.

Travel was far from easy. The forests were full of robbers ready to ambush the unwary. Mountains were difficult to cross in the winter weather between November and March, despite the presence of monastic communities living on their heights, ready to come to the aid of travelers. People always had to be on their guard against bandits, and avoid places where a war was going on. Merchants, who needed to travel quickly, rarely covered more than thirty miles a day. It took two weeks to travel from Bologna to Avignon, twenty-two days from the Champagne fairs to Nîmes, eleven or twelve days from Florence to Naples.

Sea travel was faster. With fair winds, a ship could cover as much as seventy-five miles in twenty-four hours. But the waves were also fraught with perils, from storms to pirates. The French historian Joinville, who accompanied St. Louis on his crusade, commented dryly on the foolhardiness of the "merchant adventurers": "I reflected that he is truly senseless who puts himself in such peril with the goods of other people, or in a state of mortal sin; for one goes to sleep in the evening not knowing whether one will find oneself at the bottom of the sea next morning." In the lives of the saints, many stories are told of a holy man appeasing the stormy waves. In *La légende dorée* (*The Golden Legend*), a collection of the lives of the saints, Jacobus de Voragine writes of St. Nicholas: "One day some sailors, finding themselves in peril on the sea, prayed to the saint, who appeared to them and said, 'You have called me, here I am!' And he set about helping them with the sails, ropes, and other ship's tackle, and at once, the tempest ceased."

But all these obstacles did not deter some travelers from adventuring quite far on land and sea. The Venetian Marco Polo (1254–1324) lived in China for fifteen years. His colorful account of his Far Eastern travels was widely read.

In the thirteenth century the heavy steering oar was replaced by the rudder. This made it possible to build much bigger ships, like this one with its large forecastle and afterdeck and three masts up to 145 feet high. Galleons like this, which could carry from 500 to 1000 tons, were not easy to maneuver and were used to transport heavy cargoes of little value. Ships this size could only get into a few ports—Genoa, Savona, and Majorca. Elsewhere, they had to cast anchor in the open sea; the men and cargo were then ferried ashore.

At the beginning of the Middle Ages, the maintaining and building of bridges was a religious task, often carried out by the Church or by special orders of monks. Later, the task was taken over by local lords and town magistrates. The bridges were often heavily fortified, as was Valentré bridge at Cahors, France, shown here, which was built in the fourteenth century.

Almost all over the West the excellent network of Roman highways had vanished. People had to travel on badly paved or dirt roads, plodding through mud in rainstorms or choking with dust in the heat.

Merchants, pilgrims, beggars, wandering scholars, brigands, knights errant, and itinerant monks were all to be found on the roads and highways.

MARKETS AND FAIRS

For centuries medieval trade simply consisted of bartering luxury products like fabrics, dyes, and spices, and other basic necessities like salt. In the tenth century, bulk goods, cereals, and wood slowly entered into the circuits of major commerce, and goods relating to the wool and fabric industry were increasingly sold. Great trading routes were set up between Flanders and Italy, Germany and Venice, London and the Mediterranean, and even Cordova and Kiev! Cities, ports, and riverside towns at the crossroads of these highways profited from this growth in trade. Merchants met regularly at the same fairs—the fairs of Champagne in the eleventh to thirteenth centuries and the Lendit fair on the road linking Paris to the Abbey of St. Denis. A thirteenth-century poet has left us a description that is typical of many European fairs and markets: ''First of all, there are the hucksters who sell food to the public, the beer-sellers, the publicans, and then the weavers. Not far off are the drapers, and then the parchment sellers' pitch. Then comes the open space where they sell uncured skins and wool . . . Here come people leading animals—cows, oxen, ewes, and pigs, and men selling horses, the best you can buy, mares, foals and palfreys, suitable for counts and kings.''

In northern Europe a huge confederation of ports and trading towns dominated the markets. This confederation led to the creation of the Hanseatic League, which flourished from the end of the thirteenth to the second half of the fifteenth century. The league created powerful bonds between its seventy towns. Among them, Lübeck, Hamburg, Bremen, Cracow, Breslau, and Cologne were major powers. Eventually the league became a real political force, controlling the Baltic Sea and The Sound (the strait near Denmark connecting the Kattegat with the Baltic). At its outer limits were four important trading stations in London, Bruges, Bergen, and Novgorod, which were virtually independent of the local authorities. They governed themselves according to German law and according to the directives of the Diet, the Hanseatic League's supreme body, whose delegates were supposed to meet at Lübeck every three years.

In the south, the Italians sailed the Mediterranean Sea. In the fifteenth century the Venetians, Genoans, Pisans, Sienese, and Florentines began to link East and West with their trade in precious spices, such as pepper and cinnamon. They established regular routes overland and, more importantly, by sea: merchant fleets linked Genoa and Venice to London and Bruges. Even today it is not surprising to find Flemish tapestries in Italian palaces or a statue of the Virgin by Michelangelo in a Bruges church.

In western Europe in the Middle Ages, fur was an essential, almost common clothing material. Some furs were valuable—lynx, leopard, fox, marten, and sable—but there were also cheap skins like cat and squirrel. The main production area was eastern Europe, particularly Russia. The city of Novgorod, on the trading route linking the Baltic to the Black Sea, was the major European fur market until the fifteenth century. Fur was not only a protection against the cold but also a symbol of social status. Two kings of France, Philip the Bold in 1270 and Philip the Fair in 1294, set up regulations for wearing fur, according to rank for the nobility and according to wealth for the middle classes. Furriers were classed as superior artisans, since they handled these noble and valuable materials.

THE FAIRS OF CHAMPAGNE

In the twelfth and thirteenth centuries six great fairs were held annually in the French province of Champagne; they constituted the biggest commercial and financial market of the West. They went on all through the year: from December through January at Lagny; during Lent at Bas sur Aube; in May, June, and September in Provins; and from June to July and from October to November at Troyes. Merchants from Italy, the Netherlands, Lorraine, Germany, England, and France met there regularly, where the Western trading routes crossed. They were under the patronage of the counts of Champagne, who founded the Hôtel-Dieu—a hospital—for them at Provins. The commercial activities of these great trading centers was brought to an end by the Franco-Flemish wars at the beginning of the fifteenth century, followed by the Hundred Years' War.

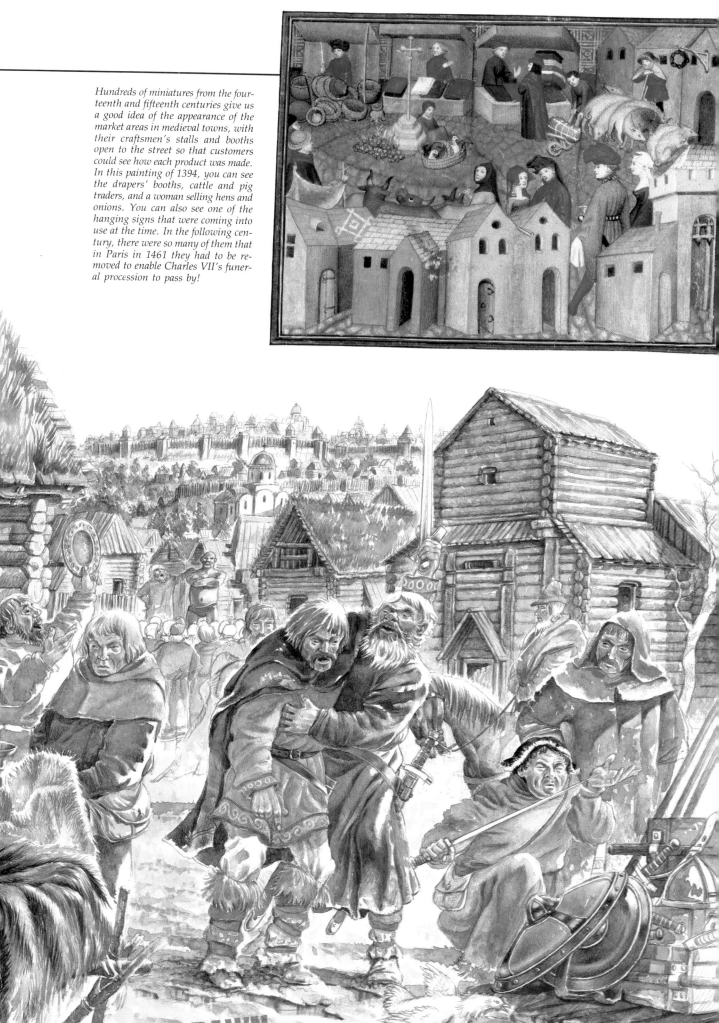

Hundreds of miniatures from the four-teenth and fifteenth centuries give us a good idea of the appearance of the market areas in medieval towns, with their craftsmen's stalls and booths open to the street so that customers could see how each product was made. In this painting of 1394, you can see the drapers' booths, cattle and pig traders, and a woman selling hens and onions. You can also see one of the hanging signs that were coming into use at the time. In the following cen-tury, there were so many of them that in Paris in 1461 they had to be re-moved to enable Charles VII's funer-al procession to pass by!

REGROWTH

In the thirteenth century, in the wake of advances in agriculture, towns enjoyed unprecedented prosperity. With their royal palaces and princes' castles, they were the centers of political power. Those with universities acquired cultural prestige, and it is significant that although the first monasteries were set up in the countryside, the mendicant (begging) orders of the thirteenth century—the Franciscans and Dominicans—established themselves in towns.

Fairs, markets, crafts, and workshops also contributed to the role of medieval cities as vital centers of trade and technological progress. At Bologna the first machine for spooling silk was invented. The technology of weaving was being improved all over Europe, producing fabrics with complex and subtle designs. Stimulated by the presence of a wealthy aristocracy and middle class, goldsmiths, jewelers, furriers, and hat and glove makers expanded the luxury goods trade. Similar progress was made in arms manufacture and furniture making. The towns also profited from advances in the mining industry and copper and silver refining.

The world of money also changed. From now on, the merchants' horizons stretched from England to the Black Sea, from Barcelona to Novgorod. Businesses like milling, metallurgy, and shipping became too costly to be one-man enterprises. Several merchants would pool their capital so that it could bear fruit. Businessmen had to be capable of playing the money market, and had to know how to make a deal in Florence and get paid in Bruges or Lyons. Because transporting sacks of coins over great distances was impractical and dangerous, the Italian invention of the bill of exchange became a means of settling business at a distance. The bill of exchange was a negotiable draft presented at a bank for payment in currency. Bankers went to other countries to buy bills of exchange. Thus, for example, an English banker would go to Rome to buy bills of exchange to be used by Roman merchants to do business in London. These merchants were paid in bills of exchange, which were later exchanged for local currency at a bank in Rome.

At the beginning of the fourteenth century, the procedure sped up; the international business world became conscious of its solidarity and the need for mutual trust. In Florence a simple signed letter began to be accepted as an acceptable means of transferring money from one individual's account to another's. The check had been invented. In Genoa the Casa de San Giorgio was a state bank, where Genoese of all social and professional classes could open accounts in which to keep their money. They could make deposits, which could be left to accumulate interest. The modern bank was well underway.

As cities achieved near independence from the power of the lords, their bell towers came to symbolize their wealth and pride. Some were magnificent, like those at Bruges, Ypres, and Arras. Some had large clocks built into them, like the tower of the Signoria Palace in Florence, built in 1354. Others were more modest, like this fifteenth-century belfry at Vaison-la-Romaine in France.

Despite the wars and plagues that weakened the West in the fourteenth and fifteenth centuries, the homes of the rich became increasingly comfortable. Their wealth took visible form in both furniture and household articles. Their rooms were filled with carved furniture, the floors were often parquet, and the ceilings were supported by elegant beams.

More and more uses were found for glass, which changed many aspects of living. Glass replaced oiled paper in the windows; in 1448 Enea Silvio Piccolomini, the future Pope Pius II, observed that half the houses in Vienna had glass windows. But glass had many other uses. It was used to make bottles, vases, mirrors, containers of all sizes—and soon, spectacles to correct shortsightedness. This invention became common in the fifteenth century, and the making of spectacles became a Florentine speciality. (The Master of Flémalle, Sainte Barbe, fifteenth century.)

The money changer was a very important person in medieval Europe. His business was to weigh and change foreign coins, using a set of small, very accurate scales. Every state wanted to be sure that it had good quality coinage; the value of silver was expressed in deniers, and gold in carats. The most valuable coins were 12 deniers and 24 carats.

The use of coins and the birth of banking gradually did away with the Church's injunctions against making money by usury and charging interest on loans—despite the fact that the Lateran Council in 1215 had condemned moneylending for profit.

THE HUNDRED YEARS' WAR

The English kings, who held the French province of Aquitaine in fief, did not enjoy being vassals of the French monarchs and having to pay them homage. The French kings, for their part, wanted to get the English out of French territory. In 1336, on the death of Charles IV, king of France, the situation came to a head.

Charles had no direct heirs, and his next of kin was the young king of England, Edward III. The French barons wanted a more distant relative, Philip of Valois, as their king. The following year, Edward threw a challenge at "him who calls himself King of France," and opened hostilities. Punctuated by many armistices, military operations were to last until 1454!

In the Hundred Years' War, most of the confrontations involved small troops of soldiers. The only large battles were Crécy in 1346, Poitiers ten years later, and Agincourt in 1415, in which thousands of men took part. In these great English victories, two different concepts of warfare came into play. The French nobility believed in following the code of chivalry, which depended on individual acts of heroism. But the English kings, chose, much more effectively, to organize and coordinate the action of their horsemen, archers, and footsoldiers.

In 1360 Edward III's armies occupied almost a third of the French kingdom. During the years that followed, the new French king, Charles V, and his constable, Bertrand du Guesclin, recovered most of these conquests. But the situation was once more reversed when France was torn apart by a civil war.

In 1392 King Charles VI went insane. His uncles, the dukes of Burgundy and Orleans, fought each other for power and contested the rights of the dauphin, the king's son. The English king Henry V was able to take advantage of their rivalry; after his victory at Agincourt, he had himself recognized as heir to the French crown. His successor, Henry VI, opposed the dauphin, and claimed a legitimate right to the French throne.

This dynastic quarrel and the war, which was renewed more fiercely then ever, seemed as if they would never end. Then Joan of Arc appeared on the scene. With her help, the former dauphin, Charles VII, supported by a reorganized army, was able to end the conflict that had devastated entire provinces. By 1453 only Calais was in the hands of the English.

The great English victories at Crécy, Poitiers, and Agincourt were due to the skill of the English and Welsh archers. Every time, their deadly storm of arrows halted the disorganized charge of the French cavalry. The chronicler of the Battle of Crécy wrote: "They drew so well that the horses, confronted by these astonishing barbed arrows, refused to advance, or leaped backwards . . . others fell down, and the English lords who were on foot advanced and struck those who could not use their horses to help them."

The Black Prince, son of Edward III; after his victory at Poitiers he ravaged the south of France, killing cattle, burning and looting as he passed. He was given his nickname both because of his cruelty and the color of his armor.

Joan of Arc, called the "Maid of Orléans," was born at Domrémy-la-Pucelle. At the age of twelve she claimed that heavenly voices had given her the mission of "driving the English out of France." At the head of a small army, she delivered Orléans, beleaguered by the enemy. In 1429 she achieved her aim of leading the dauphin to Reims, to be consecrated as the true king of France, Charles VII. Two years later she was handed over to the English by the Burgundians; she was tried and condemned for heresy and witchcraft and burned at the stake. (A sketch drawn by a clerk on the notes made at her trial.)

Looted by soldiers and mercenaries turned brigands, fought over by rival local lords, and the scene of peasants in revolt against cruel repression, the French countryside became a picture of desolation. The Italian poet Petrarch wrote: ''I found it hard to believe that this land was the one I had seen before, so greatly was it dominated by solitude, sadness, and devastation, so terrifying and bare were the fields, so ruined and deserted the houses.''

THE GREAT PLAGUE

The germs of a horrible disease, the bubonic plague—later called the "Black Death"—were brought to Europe on merchant ships, from the Genoese trading stations of the Crimea, on the Black Sea coast. Carried by fleas from infected rats that lived in the ships' holds, the plague reached its first ports of call, Constantinople, Naples, and Marseilles, in the year of 1347. Gradually the epidemic traveled northward. In the spring of 1348 death struck Florence, Milan, and Venice, and by the summer, Spain, Aquitaine, Lyons, and Paris. Within a few months, the whole of Europe was affected.

The disease was recognized by the buboes (black boils) that appeared in the victim's groin and armpits. These were speedily followed by fever, thirst, delirium, and a fixed stare. Within a few hours, the victims would die, some dropping dead in the street. A person who was perfectly fit in the morning could be dead by evening. Fear and silence fell on the towns and villages. Windows and doors were bolted. Some people no longer went outdoors. Others, by contrast, fled in aimless groups, crazed by terror.

No one was safe. Up to a point the chief victims of disease had been small children; now, young adults succumbed by hundreds of thousands, by millions. The poor and unsanitary quarters of towns, with their crowded tenements, were the first to suffer, but death also stalked through palaces, monasteries, the countryside, and remote hamlets. But it did not strike everywhere with equal force. Whole provinces, including Bohemia, Flanders, and Béarn, were spared. One village might never be touched by the plague, while another, just a few miles away, would be wiped from the face of the countryside.

No one understood the mechanics of infection, and few precautions were taken against the disease. Many people believed the plague came from a putrefaction of the air, which could be purified by burning aromatic herbs. Some blamed the arrival of a comet, and others believed the water had been poisoned. In order to appease the wrath of heaven, many people did public penance, as did the flagellants of northern Europe, who tore their own backs with leather whips tipped with iron. Scenes of madness and despair were abundant.

The French chronicler Froissart later declared that "a third part of the world" had died. And Jean de Venette concluded that the number of victims was "such as had never been heard of, nor read of, nor seen, in past times." At Castres and Albi in France half the population died or fled. In Germany the plague removed 50 percent of the population of Magdeburg, and 70 percent of Bremen. According to historians, the proportion of deaths caused by the plague in different regions was between one-eighth and two-thirds of the population.

As suddenly as it had arrived, the plague departed. The stunned survivors, after weeks of terror, recovered their taste for living. They married and had children, creating new lives as if the better to drive away death. But the vast number of births that took place in the year following the mass dying did not make up for the losses. Moreover, the plague was to attack again, sometimes mildly, sometimes with violence, every ten or twenty years. In any province, town, or village—anywhere—the plague could revive for a time and then burn itself out again.

The ravages wreaked by the plague can still be read about in some fourteenth-century archives. In parish registers, it is possible to follow the terrifying mortality rate, month by month. The curé of Givry in Burgundy recorded 39 deaths in 1345, 25 in 1346, 42 in 1347, and 649 from the beginning of January to mid-November 1348, 615 of those between August 2 and November 19. Accounts of the epidemic can also be found in the works of writers. The Italian Boccaccio described the plague in Florence in his Decameron: *"The disaster had put so much fear into the hearts of men and women that brother deserted brother, the uncle his nephew, the sister her brother, and even the wife her husband . . . Fathers and mothers, as if their children were no longer theirs, avoided going to see them and help them."*

The plague and the millions of deaths it caused made many Christians believe that the end of the world was near, that the time of the Apocalypse had come. Ancient fears were revived, like those illustrated three centuries earlier in this manuscript from the Abbey of St. Séver. In many places, people painted pictures of The Dance of Death, in which men and women of all walks of life were dragged into an infernal round dance by grinning skeletons. This theme had existed before the epidemic of 1348, but after the plague had decimated Europe it was widely reproduced. The Church, disorientated by the scourge, tried to account for it as the wrath of God, and Pope Clement VI held a special mass against the plague: "All those who hear it must carry in their hand a lighted candle for five consecutive days, after which they then cannot be struck dead." (Manuscript of Beatus de Leibana, Explanation of the Apocalypse, eleventh century, Bibliothèque Nationale, Paris.)

ITALIAN CULTURE

In the fourteenth century, although affected by the plague and frequently torn by conflicts between rival cities, Italy was seen by the rest of Europe as the land of business and the arts, of free cities and rich merchants, of scholars and philosophers.

Venice, that superb city anchored on the Adriatic, was one of the great European powers. Since the Fourth Crusade in 1202, it had headed a veritable colonial empire. Banners bearing its emblem, the lion of St. Mark, fluttered above Ragusa, Zara, Corfu, and particularly Crete. The city even owned a section of Constantinople, where it had its own government, church, and shops. Venetian trading centers were established at Lapozzo in Armenia and Alexandria in Egypt, and in Syria. And on Italian soil, Venice was mistress of the cities of Verona, Padua, and Trier, and the provinces of Friuli and Istria. Her merchant ships traded with all the Mediterranean and Atlantic ports. However, the Turkish threat looming in the East was soon to topple her from her position as the greatest port in Europe. Little by little the Venetian trading stations on the coasts of the Black Sea fell into the hands of the Turkish invaders. Moslem ships interrupted communications, and the fall of Constantinople in 1453 heralded the end of Venetian domination over the eastern Mediterranean.

The Genoese, too, were tough sailors and brilliant businessmen. They competed with Venice in a number of markets, and were to be found in England, France, Antwerp, Bruges, Lisbon, and even on the island of Madeira, off the coast of Morocco, where they developed sugar cane plantations. Their influence extended over Spanish Castile, a region in north and central Spain, and as far as the Canaries, a group of islands off the coast of Africa. This was an important factor in the life of a Genoese sailor called Christopher Columbus.

While Italy's great ports were Venice and Genoa, its artistic and intellectual capital was Florence, where the culture was supported by a remarkable economy. Florentine bankers were famous throughout Europe, and even made loans to kings. Its textile workers produced the finest fabrics; its silks and woolens were sold throughout Europe. Its painters, sculptors, jewelers, and goldsmiths created pure works of art.

And of the Italian cities where the Renaissance was soon to blossom, Milan was also flourishing. There was a brilliant court at Ferrara, and in Rome popes ruled who were interested in art and culture and the classical heritage of antiquity.

On a wall in the public palace of Siena, Ambrogio Lorenzetti painted this idealized picture illustrating how human activities lead to happiness under the leadership of wise and good rulers. It shows the countryside of Tuscany, with its variety of crops, its merchants, farms, and tree-covered hillsides. All these are depicted with an understanding of perspective, which was one of the great innovations of Italian painting. (Ambrogio Lorenzetti, The Effect of Good Government on the Countryside, 1338–1339, Palazzo Pubblico, Siena.)

TRADES IN FLORENCE

Florence's wealth was due to its thousands of workers, craftsmen, and businessmen. They were grouped in Arti, trade corporations that regulated the production and sale of most of their products. They included seven "Major Arts." The Arte di Calimala was the weavers' and cloth-makers' guild, the Arte del Cambio, the guild of the money changers and bankers. The Arte Por San Maria controlled silk manufacture. There were also Arti for wool workers, doctors and chemists, furriers, judges, and lawyers. Alongside the Major Arts were fourteen Minor Arts, including butchers, wine merchants, rope makers, tanners, and smiths. But underlying this apparent solidarity, the relations between masters and workers, artisans and waged workers, were often extremely tense. This gave rise to strikes and revolts and to demonstrations like the demonstration of the Ciompi in 1378, when the populo minuto (the working people) rose up violently against the populo grasso (the middle classes).

The Italian businessman—the banker—was fired by curiosity for all kinds of subjects. Besides speaking several languages, he was interested in books, art, music, and science. He was fascinated by anatomy and cartography, the accurate mapping of the world, sea, and skies. He placed importance on the exact measurement of time, and more and more public clocks began to appear from the fourteenth century on.

Before it became the home of art, Italy was the land of the craftsman. Never had there been so many jewelers, goldsmiths, and sculptors as in the fourteenth and fifteenth centuries.

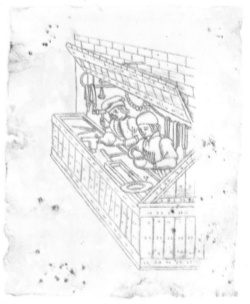

A NEW WORLD

People were weary of misfortune. The combination of the plague, famine, and warfare had laid waste to whole regions. In the fourteenth and fifteenth centuries, hundreds of villages were wiped out, leaving only the overgrown ruins of castles, farms, and churches. But this terrible depletion of resources left the survivors with a new world to rebuild, a world with an important and interesting future.

Whenever the disease abated and there was a lull in warfare and pillage, commercial activities resumed. There was trade in salt, cereals, and food products. Brittany sent vegetables to England, and in 1453 the well-to-do inhabitants of Poitiers were importing their lettuce seeds from Milan; wine and beer traveled across Europe, and the great German brewing industry started up in the fifteenth century.

On the route between Flanders and Italy, and via the Mediterranean and the Atlantic, merchants bought and sold woolens and cloths, silks and spices, leathers and linens. Between central Europe and Venice there was trade in German mineral ores—gold, silver, iron, copper, lead, and zinc—and in furs from Russia and the north, in Venetian glass, cotton fabrics, and Greek wines. Hard on the heels of trade, the world of capital was coming into its own. The Medicis in Florence, the Fugger family in Augsburg, and the French banker Jacques Coeur in France were representative of the new middle class of financiers. They became not only bankers but advisers to princes, and it was they who were responsible for the economic revival. Some rose to positions of power in their own right.

Another sign of progress was in the dissemination of news. In 1357, scarcely ten years after the great plague, seventeen Florentine companies founded the *Scarcella dei Mercanti Fiorentini*, which sent a weekly courier to Avignon, via Genoa, and back. The first known postal company, it also took private letters for a fee. At the end of the fifteenth century, in the Germanic Holy Roman Empire, a postal network was organized by the lords of Thurn und Taxis.

In agriculture, developments were even more positive. Methods of fertilization were improved. More and more herds grazed on natural or man-made pasture lands and in meadows. In Holland and Zeeland, the use of the windmill spread; it was no longer used just for milling grain. In 1408 the first water-pumping mill was used to drain the land.

After its winter of death and disasters, the West enjoyed a better life, pleasanter for nearly everyone and positively luxurious for some. In the towns the shortage of labor caused by the plague led to higher wages. In the countryside, rich fallow lands lay ready for cultivation. The living profited from the inheritance of all those who had died.

But, living amid the cruel alternation of catastrophes and renewal, between ever-present death and the will to live, the men and women of the fourteenth and fifteenth centuries were full of doubts, fears, and uncertainties. For they were still Christian; they knew that their bodies were mortal. And the human skeleton, denuded of flesh, was painted in countless pictures of the Dance of Death, and sculpted on tombs. Hell and the Devil were as menacing as ever.

At the end of the Middle Ages, clothes became important symbols of social status. The wealthy middle classes enjoyed displaying their new power by wearing sumptuous garments of wool, silk, and fur, and shoes of fabric or leather. Paris was already the home of fashion, and of polite Western manners.

Progress in shipbuilding, the invention of the rudder, which enabled ships to sail into the wind, the use of maritime maps and the compass—all these developments were to contribute to the eventual discovery of the New World. The Portuguese prince Henry II, the Navigator, was one of its moving forces. In 1416, from his base at Sagres, Cape St. Vincent, he began sending expeditions of discovery to Madeira, the Azores, the Río de Oro, Senegal, and Guinea. Western Europe began dreaming of what lay beyond the Atlantic horizon.

In the expanding world, nobles and princes still cultivated notions of chivalry and courtly love. Their favorite heroes were the Knights of the Round Table. Nostalgia for times gone by was so strong that kings created their own orders of chivalry—the Order of the Garter in England, of St. Michael in France, and the Golden Fleece in Burgundy. Within a select circle they acted out the values, deeds, and myths of King Arthur's knights. (Illustration from the Lancelot en prose, (The Prose Lancelot), Bibliothèque Nationale, Paris.)

PAUPERS AND VAGRANTS

This early fourteenth-century miniature shows a leper and a cripple being refused entry to a town by a vigilant watchman. The signs of their wretched state are clearly depicted: the cripple has clumsy crutches and a bleeding wound; the leper has a sore-covered face, wears a large robe and gloves, and carries a hand rattle and begging bowl.

Poor people, beggars, and vagrants had their own place in medieval society. In a world in which the Church preached poverty and humility as supreme values, these people were the living, tangible image of the suffering Christ. When a poor person knocked on a monastery door or at the castle gates, he was welcomed, lodged, and fed. Passing guests, travelers and pilgrims, were given the same treatment. Charity was a duty, and so was caring for the sick; hospitals and leprosariums were run by monks and nuns dedicated to this task. Some hospitals specialized. Such a hospital was the Quinze-Vingt (the "Fifteen-Twenty"), which still exists in Paris. It was founded by St. Louis in memory of the 300 (15 × 20) knights who had accompanied him on his Crusade and whose eyes had been put out by Saracens. Hospitals were usually built at the crossings of the great pilgrimage routes, at the entrance to towns, on mountain slopes, and at river crossings. At river crossings the hospital brethren's duties included the maintenance of the bridge or providing a ferry service. With the exception of leprosariums, however these institutions never received lepers. They were universally rejected, feared, and excluded, and had to warn people of their approach by ringing a bell.

As the Middle Ages went by, people came to fear all the wanderers, pilgrims, and beggars who traveled the roads. Voices were raised against them. Even pilgrims were criticized, since their "only advantage is that they have seen some pleasant views or fine monuments, or have acquired the vainglory they desire." Little by little, feelings changed toward the poor and homeless; the lords and bishops felt threatened. In fourteenth-century towns, it became impossible to distinguish between genuine paupers and the bands of vagabonds that gathered in "courts," associations of professional beggars. They were skilled at cutting the strings of purses filled with gold or silver pieces, and exploited people's compassion by faking wounds and sores and wrapping themselves in bloodstained rags. The authorities made efforts to contain these thieves and vagabonds. Beggars were ordered to leave town or find work; those who did not conform ran the risk of being beaten, branded with hot irons, or having an ear cut off. Vagrants were often ill-treated, locked up in chains at night, and forced to work by day at such tasks as cleaning the streets.

At the end of the fifteenth century Jacques Coeur, financial adviser to Charles VII of France, sent vagrants to the galleys to save honest citizens from contact with wanderers who were now seen as fodder for the gallows. At the end of the Middle Ages, while the Church continued to assist the needy, some people began to see imprisonment as the solution to the problem of poverty.

JUSTICE

In the Middle Ages the execution of justice was accompanied by a whole program of public spectacles—trial by combat or ordeal, public mutilations, and hangings. The purpose of these public spectacles was mainly to intimidate people. With no written evidence and badly kept prisons, medieval justice was a fairly primitive affair. Just the same, it was not always as cruel as is sometimes believed.

Very often, how the law was executed was primarily a question of money, which was divided between rival nobles. Some lords held the right of the "high justice" and others of the "low justice," entitling them to deal with misdemeanors only. So in one village, not all the peasants would appear before the same judge, and the rivalry between the judicial lords meant that trials could be dragged out for a long time.

In order to make up a part of their sometimes excessive expenses, kings and lords decided to impose monetary fines rather than corporal punishments. Such fines brought in even more than their tenants' land rents. With the same object in view, they spent next to nothing on the upkeep of prisons and prisoners; suspects and prisoners on parole were required to present themselves for trial on a certain day, with their possessions serving as a pledge. In a minority of cases, customs still survived from the barbarian world. Disputes were decided by ordeal, a physical test whose outcome would indicate God's judgment, since, as St. Augustine had taught, "God defends the just man." Trial by combat, in which the two people disputing a case would fight until one was dead, was regulated by the public authorities. Trial by fire—walking over hot coals without getting burned, for example—was strongly disapproved of by the Church, since it excluded any moral judgment of the individuals concerned. However, when someone was condemned to be flogged, people crowded to watch. The victim, stripped naked, with a rope around his neck, would be dragged for several days through the streets and beaten with rods in the public squares.

Forgiveness and Torture

In the twelfth century, corporal punishments began to be replaced by public acts of humiliation, in which the accused man knelt down and cried out several times for those he had wronged to forgive him. From then on, this type of punishment became common practice. Dueling, which had provided public spectacles but little justice, was from this time on confined to members of the aristocracy, for serious questions of honor. At the same time, there was an increase in the number of law courts and less recourse to trial by ordeal.

Torture, however, was often used to obtain quick confessions, particularly in cases of alleged heresy and sorcery. How it was used varied considerably between regions, provinces, and countries. It was practiced mercilessly under some jurisdictions, and unknown under others. Sometimes torture could be extremely brutal, and victims were left crippled for life. It was even used for minor transgressions. In the Paris region, for instance, at the beginning of the fifteenth century, a man accused of theft was "put to the question" nine times in three days. Judges considered that torture made justice more effective. Very few questioned its use, and it continued in many countries until the eighteenth century.

At the end of the Middle Ages, it was common practice to use torture for forcing suspects to confess. Various unpleasant techniques were applied. One was to force the victim to drink huge quantities of water, as illustrated here by Brueghel (1525–1569) in an engraving symbolically illustrating the theme of justice. (Bibliothèque Royale, Brussels.)

WOMEN IN THE MIDDLE AGES

Medieval society was dominated by fighting men, and for a long time women's lives were very restricted. At the beginning of the twelfth century, Bishop Gilbert of Limerick summed up their role as follows: "They are the wives of those who pray, those who fight and those who work, and they serve them." Serving was synonymous with total subservience to the lord and master. According to many customs prevailing at the time, serfdom was inherited through the female side. The children of a bondwoman would be serfs, even if their father was a freeman.

Among peasants, a strict division of labor allocated to women the care of the vegetable garden and small animals, weeding the crops in spring, and spinning and weaving wool. In towns, working-class women made up most of the wretched labor force of the textile industry. The poet Chrétien de Troyes wrote of them: "Always silken cloth shall we weave, and not be better dressed; always poor and naked shall go, and always hunger and thirst."

Although more is known about them as individuals, noble ladies did not have a much easier time. They were confined to women's quarters, often kept apart from a world they barely glimpsed through the castle windows. They only left home to get married, and marriage was their main function. To the medieval nobility, carrying on the family line was of prime importance. Therefore, a woman's value was increased if her marriage led to an alliance between families, and if the size of her dowry strengthened the power of the family she married into. It was also extremely important for her to ensure the continuity of the hereditary line by producing male children. In the hunt for noble wives, rich heiresses were particularly in demand. To obtain one, all means were permissible—abducting, repudiating, or disavowing an existing wife, and even incest, which the Church made efforts to stamp out by imposing its own moral rules on marriage.

Abduction and Chivalry

In 1152 Louis VII, king of France, repudiated his wife Eleanor, sole heiress to the duchy of Aquitaine. The ostensible reason was her infidelity, but, more importantly, she had failed to give him a son. As soon as she was free, the wealthy Eleanor was pursued by ambitious lords who coveted the beautiful land of Aquitaine. She just managed to escape the count of Blois and then Geoffrey Plantagenet, only to fall finally into the hands of Geoffrey's brother Henry, duke of Normandy and the future king of England. He simply seized her and took her to his bed with no formalities. Only six weeks after her repudiation, the heiress had found another master.

Although the repudiated Eleanor was able to take her dowry with her, this was unfortunately not always possible for other women. Many a woman found herself penniless after a failed marriage and had to seek her final refuge within the walls of

Widowed at twenty-five, Christine de Pisan left a moving account of the condition of women in her day: "Lonesome am I and lonesome will be, Lonesome my sweet love has left me, Lonesome am I, of my lord bereft, Lonesome am I, and friendless am left . . ." (Musée Condé, Chantilly.)

a convent. The husband often seized the dowry, as well as the marriage settlement that he was supposed to make on his wife as insurance, should she be widowed. With the same aim—to keep the family property intact—he would only marry off his eldest sons. The younger ones kicked up their heels as bachelors or devoted their lives to wandering from tournament to tournament, hoping to win fame and riches—and even, perhaps, the heart of some fair lady. Often they would dedicate themselves to a married woman, whom they served faithfully while waiting for favors that were unlikely to be granted. In the twelfth century, abduction was transformed into a kind of game controlled by the heads of families—the game of courtly love. Its purpose was to keep the young gentlemen occupied by entering them in a competition they could never win. This enabled ladies to reclaim their powers of seduction, and apparently to flout the punishments promised to adulterous wives. However, women were still seen as nothing more than the objects of masculine desire.

In the twelfth century, however, women's position slowly began to improve. The growth of the economy made it profitable for couples to produce large families. Wives had to take on greater responsibility, as evidenced by the records of property transactions that some couples signed jointly. Progress was particularly marked among the nobility. While knights went off on crusades, the chronicles tell us, their wives took charge of the castle defenses and ran their husbands' estates. These changes were echoed in fables and proverbs, which show women as talkative, nagging, and even tyrannical toward their menfolk. (Chaucer's "Wife of Bath" boasted of how she had beaten her three husbands!) But women were still often seen as instruments of the Devil: their apparent weakness was only a cover for their knowledge of secret spells and mysterious charms! As far as the Church was concerned, the only things that could neutralize their perverse nature were marriage or the religious life as nuns.

Marriage

In the Carolingian society of the eighth and ninth centuries, there were two forms of union binding men and women. There was marriage, which was only useful for in-

In Carolingian times, women seem to have been treated as lesser beings, as if in obedience to St. Paul's statement: "For the husband is head of the wife" (Eph. 5:23). For a long time, women were confined at home; however, in the Middle Ages, they began playing an important economic role. (Bibliothèque Nationale, Paris.)

heritance. There was also the regular practice of concubinage, which channeled the sexual activities of young men without endangering the "honor" of the family line. It is known that Charlemagne himself, besides having four legitimate wives, had a companion, Himiltrude, who bore him a son. Although the Church accepted this kind of union for a long time, in the twelfth century it preached monogamous marriage, and even excommunicated princes who passed lightly from one woman to another.

Until then marriage had been a private affair; now it became one of the Seven Sacraments, requiring the mutual consent of both parties. This was a major step forward for women; until then, no one had thought of asking their opinion! In contrast to the traditional image of Eve, the temptress, women were given a new image;

new, feminine figures appeared in art and sculpture, symbolizing the good Christian woman endowed with all the virtues. In cathedrals, smiling statues of the Virgin and Child were endowed with the qualities of both femininity and authority, and the cult of the Virgin Mary gave her equal status with Jesus.

In the masculine world of the Middle Ages a few women stand out. Christine de Pisan (1363–1431) succeeded in earning a living by her pen, and spent her life braving the gibes of the Parisian academics. She finally achieved recognition as the historian of the reign of Charles V. The last years of her life were spent in silent retreat, only coming out to pay tribute to the woman who had brought hope in the dark years of war—Joan of Arc. "Here is a woman, a simple shepherdess, more gallant than was any man in Rome."

MEDIEVAL MASTERPIECES

On the site of a new cathedral, the master mason would draw up the plans and direct the laborers. Then everyone set to work. The sculptor would bring a capital to life; the mason arranged the small hand-cut stones between the ribbing to support the vaulted roof one hundred feet above the floor; a craftsman set colored glass between lead strips for the windows. Build-ing a cathedral was a collective task, and we know few of the names of the artisans involved. Yet surely they deserve to be remembered!

Gothic architecture is a triumph of light, owing much to the glass industry that developed in the twelfth century. Glass-works were built near forests (which sup-plied wood for the furnaces), monasteries, and cities. There were twenty-five in France between 1207 and 1407. Making glass was a prestigious craft, for in 1373 in Nuremberg there was a glassworkers' guild to which gentlemen belonged.

Glass manufacture led to the art of making stained-glass windows. These win-dows developed along the lines recom-mended by a German monk, Theophilus, author of a technical book called *De diver-sis artibus* (*Concerning Various Arts*). His detailed instructions include descriptions of how to use a hot iron to cut out colored glass segments, how to insert them into their lead casings, and, finally, how to achieve the superb rose windows and stained-glass pictures that were the pride of the bishop-patrons. Abbot Suger, who built the Abbey of St. Denis near Paris and wanted its church to be the most resplen-dent in the West, declared that he had sought "with much care . . . the most sub-tle and exquisite masters to make painted windows . . . which cost much by the ex-cellence and rarity of the materials of which they were composed." But all this richness and luxury and profusion of color were not to everyone's taste. In the thirteenth cen-tury the Cistercians forbade the use of stained glass in their simple churches.

For most artists of the Middle Ages, nothing was too gorgeous for the glory of the Lord. Every part of a cathedral was symbolic—the building itself was the Cross; the apse, the crown of thorns; the choir, the head of Christ; the glow of the windows, the light of heaven; and the tow-ers represented arms uplifted in prayer.

Many cathedrals were decorated with rose windows, circular windows with patterns of interlacing lines. These windows are contained in the stone ribbing and the lead strips that join the pieces of stained glass.

The masterpieces of nameless craftsmen who worked in the service of the Christian faith, these windows have an other-worldly, almost unreal, quality. (La Sainte-Chapelle, 1246–1248, Paris.)

Music, the supreme art

Cathedrals, churches, and monasteries were also the places where music was played and enjoyed. Toward the end of the sixth century, Pope Gregory the Great had given the human voice a central role in the religious service, and for a long time "Gregorian chant" was one of the most moving expressions of Western spirituali-ty. Five centuries later, in the music schools attached to cathedrals, polyphon-ic works—works with two or more har-monized melodies—were composed. In-strumental music was no longer merely an accompaniment to the voice. Drums, tam-bourines, and flutes were still the most

common instruments played in popular music, but in the circles of lords and monarchs other instruments emerged—the lyre, the harp, the lute, and the viol.

Music was taught at universities in the *quadrivium*, part of the curriculum of the seven liberal arts. It was regarded as a superior branch of education and knowledge. It was said that he "who does wrong proves that he does not understand music." The organ, which had existed since antiquity, became the chief source of music for religious services in cathedrals. Harmony was studied and developed and musical notation perfected. In 1320 Philippe de Vitry published a treatise, *Ars nova* (*New Art*). This treatise described a new way of writing down music, more precise and at the same time more flexible. *Ars nova* was characterized by the poetical quality of its text and by the lyricism of its musical themes, with their intricate top line, more flowing rhythms, and freer counterpoint. The name "Ars nova" was also applied to the style of music then in fashion. In 1360 Guillaume de Machaut composed the first full polyphonic mass for four voices in this style, with the instrumental parts alternating with a variety of melodic and rhythmical themes. This *Messe Notre-Dame* (*Mass for Our Lady*) was one of the works that most influenced the late medieval composers. Ars nova swiftly spread to Flanders, Florence, and England, and then to Germany and Spain.

In the fifteenth century, royal courts began employing chapel masters. The days of the troubadours and *trouvères* of France, the English minstrels and the German *minnesaengers*, with their songs of love and the glorious past, were over.

The colors of real life

As with music, the evolution of art during the Middle Ages was to provide painters with techniques and subjects for centuries to come. Romanesque churches were already decorated with frescoes, and Byzantine paintings had given the West a taste for icons. But with the Florentine painter Giotto, the history of modern painting and the age of great masterpieces truly began. Giotto (1267–1337) used light, delicate colors, and composed simple, beautifully balanced arrangements of figures and masses, using real men and women as models. In his frescoes he moved on from the symbols customarily used in painting by introducing a humanistic realism that already heralded the Renaissance.

In the fourteenth century the art of painting was highly valued in Italy, which abounded with artists' studios. It was in Italy that in 1390 the first technical treatise appeared, covering all aspects of painting. The author advised on the use of particular colors in tempera painting: "If blue is to be used and is dark in hue, add a little glue or the yolk of an egg; but if the blue is pale, choose the yolk of a dark brown country egg. Mix it well with the pigment. Apply three or four layers to the material with a silk brush."

Elsewhere in Europe, mainly in Flanders, France, and Germany, other painters were experimenting with new techniques and styles. The Flemish painter Jan van Eyck (1422–1441) was one of the first to use oil. On a wood base primed with white lime, mixing the pigments with oil made the paint more fluid, enabling artists to correct, retouch, and make additions. This kind of perfectionism was impossible with frescoes, which required the colors to be applied very quickly to the wall before the plaster dried. Painting in oils gave pictures a new luminosity, transparence, and depth that revolutionized the history of European painting.

THE SAINTS

The saints were very much present in the medieval world as protectors and as intermediaries for sinners with Christ. From the very early days of the Church, the cult of martyrs had been solidly established in Europe, particularly in Rome. It was there, in the third century, that the Feast of St. John had replaced the pagan celebration of the summer solstice. Five centuries later, 1,300 saints were venerated with devotion in France. People squabbled over possession of martyrs' relics, and rumors of miracles drew throngs to their tombs before they had even been canonized. Canonization was at first initiated entirely by the people, and then simply sanctioned by the bishop. But this led to a number of abuses, and in the eighth century the Church reacted. In 993 the pope carried out the first official canonization of a saint. After that it was forbidden to develop a cult around a dead person without the sanction of the Church's supreme authority, the Holy See.

La légende dorée (*The Golden Legend*), written in 1264 by an Italian Dominican, Jacobus de Voragine, recounts the lives of almost two hundred Christian saints. They were the object of cults, mainly among the ordinary people, and often just within one town, region, or even trade. Nevertheless, several great figures acquired a fame that crossed many frontiers. St. George, for example, martyred in Palestine in the fourth century, was revered throughout the whole of Europe after his story was brought back by Crusaders. Churches, shrines, and altars were dedicated to him and he was patron saint of towns and villages all over France. He was especially highly thought of in England. In 1222 a national council made it obligatory to celebrate his feast day, and in the fourteenth century he became the English patron saint. Throughout Christendom, he was painted by countless artists gloriously slaying the dragon of sin.

Some people inspired enormous devotion during their lifetimes by their example of virtuous living, which appealed to the widespread urge for religious revival. One of these was St. Francis of Assisi in the thirteenth century, who called himself "God's Buffoon."

This painting by Giotto illustrates the life of St. Francis of Assisi against the backdrop of an Italian town. In keeping with the Franciscan spirit, Giotto's frescoes have a narrative style and convey a sense of realism. For the artist, as for St. Francis's disciples, it was important to demonstrate, preach, and teach the words of the Gospel and of the most illustrious Christians, by showing them at their best. (Church of St. Francis, Assisi.)

The Little Brothers

Francis, the son of a rich merchant, gave up his family and inheritance to follow in Christ's footsteps and live in utter poverty and simplicity. He went barefoot, begged for his food, and preached repentance at the Portiuncula chapel on the outskirts of Assisi. His humility attracted others, and he gathered eleven companions, "little brothers." They made no vows and had no authority other than Francis's spiritual and moral leadership; they lived in total religious freedom, based on the injunctions of the Gospels. They worked with their hands and cared for the sick and for the lepers. Gradually their fame spread through the whole of Tuscany. But their renunciation of the world was very close to the attitude of some of the heretics, and aroused the suspicions of the Church. Under pressure from the pope, the little brothers became a religious order, the Franciscans. Faithful to "Holy Poverty," Francis took himself to live as far away as he could from everything and everyone. He was almost blind when he died in 1226, and was canonized two years later at Assisi. The example of his life brought the ideal of sainthood closer to ordinary people. The thirteenth-century saints who lived and suffered in communal poverty were loved for their humanity and compassion.

THE LAST JUDGMENT

For medieval folk a comet or an eclipse was a certain sign that God was announcing His imminent return. At times of famine and at the height of the plague, everyone recalled the terrible prophecies declaimed by popular preachers:

"Oh, you who are blind, do you now flee the Day of Wrath to come, when God shall separate the sheep from the goats? Soon God will loose evil over the earth . . . Then will come the reign of the Antichrist, and the peoples seduced by his lies will turn away from God. Then heaven will grow dark, and the trumpets of judgment will sound . . . God shall appear in His glory, he will place the elect at His right hand, and at his left sinners will be thrown into the fires of hell . . ."

The fear of God's judgment came to a head in the eleventh century. In a Europe that was still profoundly ignorant, the Church exhorted people to repent. Carvings on the capitals of Romanesque churches depicted huge demons inflicting horrible tortures on the damned. In the *Apocalypse* at St. Sever, Satan has been given red eyes and hair and wings of fire.

However, in the twelfth century the fear of Hell diminished. Above the entrances of cathedrals the Last Judgment was now portrayed as the triumph of Christ in majesty, of God in His goodness rewarding the faithful and forgiving sinners. The God who triumphed over death promised human beings resurrection and the life to come. Henceforth, the fear of damnation was replaced by hope for eternal life in Paradise.

Satan and His Demons

In the fourteenth century everything changed once more. The bubonic plague, wars, and the Turkish invasion of the East were all interpreted as divine punishment. In the towns, mendicant friars and penitents preached to the populace of the punishments to come. Artists and sculptors created vivid pictures of Hell: revolting worms, toads, and snakes crawled out of the bodies of the dead; tentacled monsters dragged the tiny figures of the damned toward mysterious, steaming swamps. Sinners were stretched over grills and showered with molten lead, while demons unraveled the intestines of sinners who had been guilty of envy. Paintings by Hieronymus Bosch from the end of the fifteenth century depict these horrible nightmares: Satan, surrounded by bird-headed demons, wears a turban and rolls fiery eyes; he has rat's paws and a burning furnace in place of a belly. The damned are pierced with arrows and hang from gallows by their hands and feet. Farther off, a sinner turns the handle of an enormous hurdy-gurdy for all eternity, while another is crucified on a huge harp.

While some lived in mortal fear of damnation, others had quite a different view. Before Judgment Day arrived, they believed, Satan would be chained up for a thousand years; the last days of the world would be a period of happiness and equality for humanity. These people believed the current misfortunes heralded the approach of this Golden Age, when Christ would return to an earth free of sin.

Inspired either by hope for the new life or fear of the Apocalypse, astrologers were kept busy making calculations and predictions to find out exactly when the end of the world was due. Although the Renaissance was to bring about a new vision of life, people had never been so convinced that the world was reaching its end.

The imagination of medieval artists was stimulated by the idea of the Last Judgment, Hell, and the Devil. These themes could be found everywhere, on capitals and the fronts of churches, on manuscripts and in paintings and mosaics. Fear of the afterlife inspired the creation of monsters, grotesque creatures, horned or covered with scales, as in this eleventh-century miniature; an angel is closing the gates of Hell on the eternal suffering of the Damned. (Psalter of Henry of Blois, Manchester, The British Library, London.)

MONASTIC KNIGHTS

In the eleventh century the Church reconciled Christian ideals with the military life by turning fighting men into warriors for Christ. A passion for fighting the infidel led to the creation of orders of monastic knights.

The first was the Order of the Knights Hospitallers of St. John of Jerusalem, with its insignia of the Red Cross. Founded about 1050, its mission was to shelter and care for the poor and sick pilgrims who ar-rived in the Holy Land. Later the Crusades encouraged the order to become more military. Alongside the Hospitallers, a larger brotherhood of knights, recruited from noble families, watched over the roads and protected travelers against brigands. This concern to protect pilgrims led to the creation in 1118 of a new order, the Knights Templar. Founded by a noble from Champagne and supported by St. Bernard, the order rapidly acquired a reputation equal to that of the Hospitallers, and the nobility of Europe gave them donations of land and money. Soon thousands of men had joined these knightly orders, including "sergeants" (feudal servants who attended their masters in battle) as well as knights of noble birth.

The emblem of the Teutonic Knights was the white cloak with a black cross worn by members of the order. The brotherhood was divided into knights, priests, and servants. (Bibliothèque Nationale, Paris.)

Arms and Money

By the end of the twelfth century the Templars, Hospitallers, and Teutonic Knights had become a real military force. The Templars had eighteen huge fortresses, each protecting smaller castles and controlling hundreds of domains in both East and West. The wealth of the monastic knights increased even more with the growth of trade in the twelfth century. In the Mediterranean, their ships carried cedar, myrrh, incense, sugar cane, and spices. On land, at the Champagne fairs, the Templars controlled the entire textile trade. In Paris the citadel of the Templars housed a huge fortune. They often lent money to the king; the white-cloaked brothers had become shrewd bankers.

Soon, with the inexorable advance of Islam, the military orders had to abandon the Holy Land. Acre, the last fortress of St. John in Palestine, fell in 1291. The Hospitallers withdrew to Cyprus and the Templars dispersed throughout Europe. By that time the Teutonic Knights had already transferred most of their troops to Prussia, where they founded a kingdom. In France, Philip the Fair became envious of the Templars' financial power. He had them arrested on trumped-up charges of sorcery and heresy; under torture, they confessed to all kinds of things, which they later retracted. Some fifty knights, including the grand master, Jacques de Molay, were burned at the stake in 1310. Most of their wealth was confiscated by the king. The rest was handed over to the Hospitallers, who were resisting the Turks in Cyprus, Rhodes, and Malta. For centuries these islands were the advance posts of Christianity. The Order of the Knights of Malta, which descended from the Hospitallers, still exists, dedicated to helping and caring for the sick all over the world. The order is regarded as a sovereign state, without territory, and is recognized by some fifty countries.

This fantastic fortress in Syria belonged to the Order of Hospitallers and was built to affirm the Christian presence on Islamic soil. With its huge walls and double ramparts separated by a large water-filled moat, it has defied time as well as the ene-my. Even so, it was captured in 1271 by the sultan Baybars, but he spared the lives of the garrison.

SENTINELS OF STONE

The first castles were built on hilltops with earthen walls and wooden stockades. They were just about strong enough to protect their owners from robber bands or marauding soldiers. But should the Vikings arrive, or an army on campaign, these fragile defenses could be smashed to smithereens.

Around the year 1000, when new churches were being built everywhere, fortresses of stone began to be constructed. Much stronger, they were defenses to be reckoned with, statements of a king's or baron's power. They guarded the frontiers of provinces and were the homes of lords who were sometimes robbers themselves. Often they were all too ready to strip of their possessions any travelers, pilgrims, and rich merchants who passed through their lands.

Fortified castles were symbols of power and indications of a military presence. For the peasants who worked in the shadow of their walls, they could be menacing or protective; they were changed and adapted to the ever-developing art of war-fare. Their ramparts grew thicker, and huge keeps (heavily fortified inner towers) rose within their turreted ramparts. At first covered walkways were built in their battlements, from which stones, arrows, and boiling oil could be hurled at the enemy. These were replaced by machicolations, openings in the floors of stone parapets, which served the same purpose and were impossible to burn. The entrances were made impregnable by drawbridges over moats and heavy portcullises (iron grating suspended by chains). The whole fortification was built so that there would be no blind spots in case of an attack. Every single assailant must be permanently in view, vulnerable to the defenders' arrows; no one must be able to get near enough to the walls to put ladders against them.

These castles were also real centers of culture. Within their walls banquets, hunting parties, festivals, and military training took place, and they offered daily hospitality to guests and traveling entertainers and troubadours. In times of danger, the local villagers could take refuge there; and they paid for this protection, for it was their labor that fed the castle lords.

From the fifteenth century on, the huge walls became obsolete. With the development of artillery and the art of the siege, castles became extremely vulnerable. Even so, in southwestern France the Lord of Bonaguil built himself a masterpiece of defense, a castle bristling with watchtowers, surrounded by moats, and dominated by an enormous keep built like the stem of a ship. This vessel of stone, completely out of date, was never attacked.

Between the tenth and the fifteenth centuries the whole of the West was dotted with castles, as far as the furthermost frontiers of Christian conquest—in the Holy Land and Spain, in Greece, on the Baltic coast, in Cyprus, and in Scotland. Everywhere in Europe these stone citadels, walled towns, and fortified bridges are still to be seen. Yet what remains is only a small fraction of the number built in the Middle Ages. A great many were destroyed by war. Some were demolished by kings to bring to heel lords who had too much power for their liking. And then, of course, there were ruined lords, and families with no descendants, whose massive homes simply died, to become sources of building materials for the local peasantry.

CHRONOLOGY

	EVENTS	PEOPLE	CULTURAL EVENTS
Invasions and migrations			
	395 Separation of the Eastern and Western empires		
400	407 Germans invade Gaul		
	414 Visigoths in Spain		
	441–442 Conquest of Britain by Angles and Saxons	453 Death of Attila	
		476 Fall of the last Roman emperor	
		481 Accession of Clovis	
500			526–546 Building of San Vitale at Ravenna
		c. 534 St. Benedict writes the Rule of his Order	537 Completion of Santa Sophia at Constantinople
From the first kingdoms to the last Carolingians			
600		590–604 Gregory the Great as pope	
		622 Hegira of Mohammed	
		629–639 Reign of Dagobert, Merovingian king of the Franks	
700	711–719 Moslem conquest of Spain		
	732 Battle of Poitiers	751 Pippin the Short elected king of the Franks	773 Introduction of Arabic numerals
	793–795 Vikings attack Ireland		786 The Great Mosque built at Cordova
800	834 onward: annual Viking raids on French coasts	800 Charlemagne crowned emperor	
	843 Treaty of Verdun	861 Cyrillus and Methodius start preaching to the Bulgars	
900			910 Abbey of Cluny founded
Renewal			
		962 Otto the Great crowned emperor	
1000	1030 Communal movement starts in Italy	987 Accession of Hugh Capet	1006–1019 Church of St. Philibert de Tournus built
	1077 Canossa	1066 William of Normandy conquers England	1065 *Song of Roland* composed
	1099 Capture of Jerusalem by First Crusade		
1100		1108–1216 Innocent III as Pope	1132 Church of St. Denis built
	1148 Second Crusade fails	1155 Frederick Barbarossa Holy Roman Emperor	1160 *Tristan and Isolde*
			1163–1182 Cathedral of Notre Dame built in Paris
	1187 Saladin captures Jerusalem	1170 Murder of Thomas à Beckett	
1200	1204 Capture of Constantinople during the Fourth Crusade		1194–1260 Building of Chartres Cathedral
	1212 Battle of Las Navas de Tolosa	1206 St. Dominic preaches to the Cathari	
	1214 Battle of Bouvines	St. Francis retires from the world	
	1215 Magna Carta signed	1209–1229 Alibigensian Crusade	1232 Building of the Alhambra begun in Granada
	1271–1295 Marco Polo travels in China	1226–1270 Reign of St. Louis of France	1252–1259 St. Thomas Aquinas teaches in Paris
		1285–1314 Reign of Philip the Fair of France	
1300	1305 Papacy moves to Avignon		1296–1304 Giotto's *Life of St. Francis*
Times of trouble			
	1337 Start of Hundred Years War		
	1347–1349 Black Death in Europe		1394–1460 Henry the Navigator
1400	1410 Battle of Tannenburg	1416 Death of John Huss	
		1431 Martyrdom of Joan of Arc	
			1421–1434 The Duomo built in Florence
		1434 Cosimo de Medici ruler in Florence	
	1453 Constantinople captured by Mehmet II		1450 Gutenberg starts printing business at Mainz

INDEX

Further Reading

Atlas of Medieval Europe by Donald Matthew, Facts on File, 1982.
Medieval People by J.J. Bagley, David and Charles, 1978.
The Middle Ages by Trevor Cairns, Lerner Publications, 1974.
The Middle Ages by Alan Clifford, Greenhaven, 1980.
The Roman Empire and the Dark Ages by Giovanni Caselli, Peter Bedrick Books, 1985.

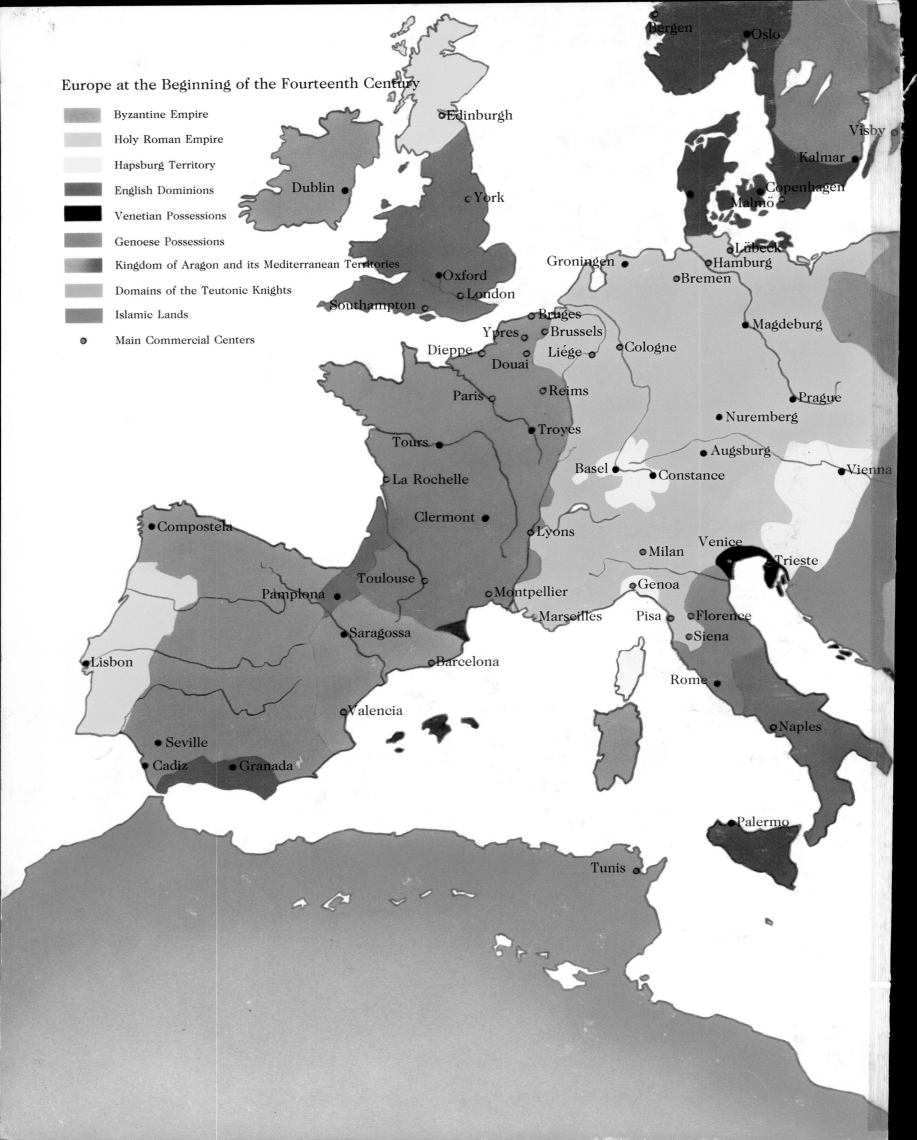

Europe at the Beginning of the Fourteenth Century

Byzantine Empire

Holy Roman Empire

Hapsburg Territory

English Dominions

Venetian Possessions

Genoese Possessions

Kingdom of Aragon and its Mediterranean Territories

Domains of the Teutonic Knights

Islamic Lands

Main Commercial Centers

Bergen
Oslo
Visby
Kalmar
Copenhagen
Malmö
Lübeck
Edinburgh
Hamburg
Groningen
Bremen
Magdeburg
Dublin
York
Bruges
Brussels
Cologne
Oxford
Ypres
Liége
London
Dieppe
Douai
Prague
Southampton
Reims
Paris
Troyes
Nuremberg
Tours
Augsburg
Basel
Vienna
La Rochelle
Constance
Clermont
Lyons
Compostela
Venice
Milan
Trieste
Toulouse
Genoa
Pamplona
Montpellier
Florence
Saragossa
Marseilles
Pisa
Siena
Lisbon
Barcelona
Rome
Valencia
Naples
Seville
Cadiz
Granada
Palermo
Tunis